DATE DUE

LIBRARIES AND THE CHANGING FACE OF ACADEMIA

responses to growing multicultural populations

by
REBECCA R. MARTIN

The Scarecrow Press, Inc.
Metuchen, N.J., & London
1994

This book is based in part on the author's dissertation, "Academic Library Responsiveness to Multicultural Student Needs," accepted as partial fulfillment of the requirements for the degree of Doctor of Public Administration at the University of Southern California, 1992.

British Library Cataloguing-in-Publication data available.

Library of Congress Cataloging-in-Publication Data

Martin, Rebecca R.
  Libraries and the changing face of academia : responses to grow-
ing multicultural populations / by Rebecca R. Martin.
    p. cm.
  Includes bibliographic references and index.
  ISBN 0-8108-2824-3 (acid-free paper)
  1. Academic libraries—United States—Services to minorities.
I. Title.
Z675.U5M3384 1994
027.6'3'0973—dc20   93-42118

For Joe

TABLE OF CONTENTS

ACKNOWLEDGEMENTS

Many people have provided the support which has made this book possible. I would like to acknowledge the committee which directed the dissertation upon which it is based, Chester Newland, John Kirlin, and Jeffrey Chapman, of the University of Southern California, whose encouragement and guidance were important in shaping this inquiry and in realizing its completion. I am indebted to Meredith Butler at the University at Albany, Allan Dyson at the University of California, Santa Cruz, and Robert Migneault at the University of New Mexico, and their respective staffs, for giving me access to their libraries and their campuses for this research. I also deeply appreciate Joseph Lubow's work in editing and preparation of camera-ready copy.

Equally important have been the many people who have helped me in my own struggle with understanding the complex issues of diversity and racism. My California colleagues Janice Koyama, Vivian Sykes, and Judith Lessow-Hurley, and those at the University of Vermont, Larry McCrorey, Juliet Young, Dalmas Taylor, Tony Chavez, Marion Metevier-Redd, Deep Ford, and Rodney Patterson all have been instrumental in this endeavor. I have learned a great deal from students of color at San Jose State University and the University of Vermont. My parents, Benjamin and Harriet Reist, have given me a strong foundation in the celebration of diversity which my husband Joseph Lubow, son Ben Martin, and I strive to make part of our daily lives.

Finally, I thank my husband and partner, Joe, for the countless hours of editing, discussing, cajoling, formatting, and reassuring he has given me on this work.

ACKNOWLEDGEMENTS

A NOTE ON LANGUAGE

The choice of terminology in referring to the United States' racial and ethnic groups is a difficult one, because language in this arena has been in transition since the early 1960s. While the term *minority* is still dominant in the literature, it carries negative connotations of exclusion and lower status. As part of efforts to develop the positive aspects of cultural pluralism on college and university campuses, many institutions are replacing the word minority with such terms as multicultural, diverse, multiethnic, and people of color. Each of these creates some problems when considered in relation to their literal meanings; however, in this usage, they have come to represent people, both as individuals and groups, who define their own heritage as coming from diverse cultural or racial backgrounds. Although these labels are necessary in distinguishing these people from those who are members of the dominant culture, no assumption should be made that values and behaviors correspond directly to race and ethnicity.

In this work, multicultural has been selected as the term now commonly used. It may be defined broadly to include race, ethnicity, class, sexual orientation, religion, gender, age, and physical ability, or specifically to refer to underrepresented racial and ethnic groups: African Americans, Hispanics, Native Americans, and Asian Americans.[1] In its latter meaning, the phrase *multicultural students* has been well established in the education literature since the early 1980s, where it is most prevalent in the literature on bilingual education at the primary and secondary levels. This term is beginning to appear in the professional literature of higher education and library science[2] and is in active use on two of the campuses studied in this research.

Another term which has become the language of choice for many members of racial and ethnic groups in the United States in the 1990s is *people of color*. This term, in addition to its derivatives *students of color* and *faculty of color*, is now accepted in the professional literature

ix

of higher education and library science. It is also used where appropriate in this work.

The newly emerging conventions regarding terminology for specific groups—African American to refer to the nation's black population, and Anglo to identify those of European extraction and to distinguish them from others of Native American/European or mixed Hispanic origin—will be used. All terms—Hispanic, Asian American, Native American, African American, and Anglo—will also be used with the understanding that they, in themselves, each represent considerable diversity.

Notes

1. Derald Wing Sue, Patricia Arrendondo and Roderick J. McDavis, "Multicultural Counseling Competencies and Standards," *Journal of Multicultural Counseling and Development* 20 (1992): 64-88; and Brenda Mitchell-Powell, "Color Me Multicultural," *MultiCultural Review* 1 (1992): 15-17.

2. See, for example, Allan J. Dyson, "Reaching Out for Outreach; A University Library Develops a New Position to Serve the School's Multicultural Students," *American Libraries* 20 (1989): 952-954; Arthur Levine, "A Time to Act," *Change* 24 (1992): 4-5; and Sue, Arrendondo and McDavis, 64-88.

PART ONE

THE CHANGING FACE OF ACADEMIA

1
THE CONTEXT FOR CHANGE

Introduction

Academic libraries on many college and university campuses are faced with the challenge of responding to the needs of increasingly diverse student populations. The compositions of these student bodies have changed dramatically in the recent past. Twenty-five years ago, it was a great deal easier to characterize "average" college students: the way they looked, the way they sounded, and the way they had been prepared to use the library.

The Cooperative Institutional Research Program reported that multicultural representation among first-year college students in 1967 was 5.7 percent.[1] By 1991, undergraduate enrollment by students of color had risen to 20.6 percent,[2] with even larger multicultural populations on many college and university campuses.

The demographic projections for the next decade make successfully meeting the needs of this diverse group of students an even greater concern. By 2010, the combined multicultural populations of the southwestern states of Arizona, California, Colorado, New Mexico, and Texas will become the numeric majority. In these states in 1989, more than 45 percent of the children under five were members of multicultural groups, primarily Hispanic.[3]

Nationwide, by the year 2000, more than one-third of all school-age children and youth will fall into this category.[4] The proportion of high school graduates who are multicultural group members is expected to rise from 22 percent in 1986 to 28 percent in 1995.[5]

Higher Education For a Diverse Nation

Higher education is a critical element in making this diversity a strength for the nation. Education has been a salient element in many prominent national reports on issues of race, ethnicity, and economics, including *One-Third of a Nation*, which asserted:

> America is moving backward—not forward—in its efforts to achieve the full participation of minority citizens in the life and prosperity of the nation....If we allow these disparities to continue, the United States will inevitably suffer a compromised quality of life and a lower standard of living.[6]

The role of education in this picture is clear, as this report went on to state:

> For more than a generation, a college education has been a key part of the American dream—and for many individuals and families, a good measure of progress toward its fulfillment. Statistics on incomes and living standards support the beliefs that college is the passport to greater opportunity and achievement.[7]

Demographic changes and economic advancement are not the only forces driving the increasing importance of higher education for the nation's multicultural populations. The nature of the workplace is changing, with increasing emphasis on information and service industries and declining numbers of manufacturing and agricultural jobs. Cleveland observed that, in 1955, 29 percent of U.S. workers were engaged in knowledge, information, and education industries. By 1975, this proportion had grown to 50 percent with indications that, by the end of the century, over two-thirds of the American workforce will be working primarily with information.[8]

In *Workforce 2000*, a 1987 report commissioned by the U.S. Department of Labor, the nature of the workforce was projected to change rapidly by the year 2000, with the fastest-growing job sectors in the professional, technical, and sales fields requiring the highest education and skill levels. Very few new jobs will be created for those who cannot read, follow directions, and use mathematics, and a majority of all new jobs will require postsecondary education. This same report indicated that people of color will make up 29 percent of the new entrants into the labor force between 1987 and 2000 and that immigrants will represent a major share of this group.[9] Education is an essential element in preparing this workforce for the changing job market.

A review of pertinent statistics indicates that higher education has not kept pace with these demographic shifts in the population and those projected for the workforce. Although enrollment levels for students of color are increasing, in 1988 they fell short of reflecting the diversity in the national population of 18- to 24-year-olds or even of that among high school graduates nationwide. The Western Interstate Commission for Higher Education and the College Board found that, although 1990 U.S. Census data indicates that 29.5 percent of the 18- to 24-year-old population were multicultural, only 22.8 percent of high school graduates in 1988 fell into this group. Participation levels in higher education dropped even further, with only 16.6

percent of undergraduates enrolled in 1988 being students of color.[10]

The Changing Student Population

After a decade of decline, 1991 multicultural enrollment figures in American colleges and universities rose 9 percent from 1990, reaching record levels for all groups other than Anglos. Overall, Anglo students accounted for 76.5 percent of the 14.3 million students enrolled in 1991, followed by African Americans at 9.3 percent, Hispanics at 8.0 percent, Asians at 4.4 percent, international students at 2.9 percent, and Native Americans at 0.8 percent.[11]

Yet the numbers of multicultural students receiving baccalaureate degrees is still disturbingly low, and attainment at the graduate level is even more dismal. In a comprehensive study of 28,000 high school seniors in 1980, Porter found that, overall, 41 percent completed the bachelor's degree within six years of high school graduation. However, the African-American and Hispanic completion rates, at 25 to 30 percent, seriously lagged behind those of Anglos and Asians, over 50 percent of whom graduated from college within six years.[12] In 1991, of the bachelor's degrees awarded by U.S. colleges and universities, 83.6 percent went to Anglos, with 6.0 percent earned by African Americans, 3.4 percent by Hispanics, 3.8 percent by Asians, 0.4 percent by Native Americans, and 2.7 percent by international students.[13]

The impact of the changing student population on educational programs and services and the growing emphasis on improving graduation rates for these students are being felt on college and university campuses across the country. In many cases, increasing the participation and success of multicultural students has become an important institutional goal.

If colleges and universities are to be successful in preparing their multicultural populations for involvement and achievement in this society, students of color must be able to work to their full potentials and eventually graduate. All students must be provided with the tools they need to succeed in the university environment so that they may acquire the education necessary to prosper in later life.

Multicultural students often differ from those who grew up within the dominant culture by language, perspective, and interests, creating barriers between their abilities and the university's expectations of student performance. The university's purpose should not be to create easy paths to success for multicultural students, but to develop successful avenues along which these students may gather the necessary skills and accomplish the goal which the university has set: to graduate with the competence necessary to compete in the broader society dominated by the majority culture, or, in some localities, a society of diversity.

Organizational Change and Diversity

Successful organizational models for dealing with diversity in higher education emphasize, among other things, the need for well-developed support services that address multicultural student needs. Such programs focus on these students, the barriers they face, and the factors associated with successful completion of their programs. Yet the library, often regarded as the heart of the university and central to its curricular programs, is seldom mentioned in strategies to improve multicultural student attainment. Though one study linked multicultural student retention to use of campus facilities, including the library,[14] programs which systematically address multicultural student needs through academic library services exist at only a few institutions nationwide.

The role of the library as a central learning resource has expanded over the past decade as higher education has turned increasingly to independent and action learning strategies.[15] In a seminal work underwritten by the Carnegie Foundation for the Advancement of Teaching, *College: The Undergraduate Experience in America*, Ernest Boyer wrote that:

> The college library must be viewed as a vital part of the undergraduate experience....The library staff should be considered as important to teaching as are classroom teachers. Since the library expresses the philosophy of education and the distinctive characteristics of a college, its role should be to bring students, faculty, and books together in ways that encourage learning, intensive scholarship, and casual browsing.[16]

The rapid development of information technology has also forced faculty into closer collaboration with librarians as those most knowledgeable in accessing the explosion of available information.[17]

Librarians have a great deal to offer students in their academic endeavors. The unique contributions of the library include a meaningful framework for the knowledge and information needed by all disciplines, an ideal environment for problem solving within a vast array of information resources, and a natural environment for lifelong learning.[18] Librarians play key roles in teaching students the problem-solving and information-seeking skills which are critical to their success. To be effective in the multicultural environment, libraries and librarians must be responsive to the variety of needs which a diverse population presents.

practical literature on library services for multicultural populations.

Part II explores the responses to multicultural student needs by libraries at three public universities in different parts of the United States. In-depth case studies are presented for library programs at the University of California, Santa Cruz, the University of New Mexico, and the University at Albany, State University of New York.

Part III provides an analysis of the program approaches used at the case study sites, considering libraries as public organizations and drawing from the organizational responsiveness literature. Advantages and disadvantages of these programs are identified and models for development of response to multicultural student needs in other settings are presented. A library agenda for change is also offered.

Notes

1. In Alexander W. Astin, *Minorities in American Higher Education* (San Francisco: Jossey-Bass, 1982), 80.

2. Jean Evangelauf, "Number of Minority Students in College Rose 9% from 1990 to 1991, U.S. Reports," *Chronicle of Higher Education*, 20 January 1993, A30.

3. Morgan Odell and Jere J. Mock, eds. *A Crucial Agenda: Making Colleges and Universities Work Better for Minority Students* (Boulder, CO: Western Interstate Commission for Higher Education, 1989), 1.

4. American Council on Education, *One-Third of a Nation; a Report of the Commission on Minority Participation in Education and American Life* (Washington, DC: American Council on Education and Education Commission of the States, 1988), 1.

5. Western Interstate Commission for Higher Education and The College Board, *The Road to College; Educational Progress by Race and Ethnicity* (Boulder, CO: Western Interstate Commission for Higher Education, 1991), 3-4.

6. American Council on Education, 1.

7. Ibid., 13.

8. Harlan Cleveland, *The Knowledge Executive* (New York: E.P. Dutton, 1985), 27.

9. William B. Johnston, *Workforce 2000; Work and Workers for the 21st Century* (Indianapolis, IN: Hudson Institute, 1987), 75-103.

10. Western Interstate Commission for Higher Education and the College Board, 16, 22, 28, 36, 42.

11. Evangelauf, A30.

12. Oscar F. Porter, *Undergraduate Completion and Persistence at Four-Year Colleges and Universities* (Washington, DC: National Institute of Independent Colleges and Universities, 1990), 12.

13. U.S. Department of Education, "Bachelors Degrees Conferred by Racial and Ethnic Group, 1990-91," *Chronicle of Higher Education*, 2 June 1993, A25.

14. Brent Mallinckrodt and William F. Sedlacek, "Student Retention and the Use of Campus Facilities by Race," *NASPA Journal* 24 (1987): 28-32.

15. Maureen Pastine and Linda Wilson, "Curriculum Reform: The Role of Academic Libraries," in *The Evolving Educational Mission of the Library*, ed. Betsy Baker and Mary Ellen Litzinger (Chicago: Association of College and Research Libraries, 1992), 98.

16. Ernest L. Boyer, *College: The Undergraduate Experience in America* (New York: Harper and Row Publishers, 1987), 164.

17. Pastine and Wilson, 100.

18. Hannelore Rader and William Coons, "Information Literacy: One Response to the New Decade," in *The Evolving Educational Mission of the Library*, ed. Betsy Baker and Mary Ellen Litzinger (Chicago: Association of College and Research Libraries, 1992), 111.

19. Harlan Cleveland, "Theses of a New Reformation: The Social Fallout of Science 300 Years after Newton," *Public Administration Review* 48 (1989): 685.

20. Mary Timney Bailey, "Minnowbrook II: An End or a New Beginning?" *Public Administration Review* 49 (1989): 224.

21. Phoebe Janes and Ellen Meltzer, "Origins and Attitudes: Training Reference Librarians for a Pluralistic World," *Reference Librarian* no. 30 (1990): 146.

2
CULTURAL DIVERSITY
IN HIGHER EDUCATION

Overview

One of the major challenges facing institutions of higher education today is to find ways to increase the levels of enrollment and success of multicultural students. For years, researchers have forecast increasing diversity among students in higher education as a result of changing demographics and a variety of other social and economic shifts. During the late 1980s, there was a decided change in the statements of concern by politicians, educators, and demographers who began to look upon the lack of multicultural achievement in education as a significant barrier to the full participation of people of color in many aspects of American life.

Major societal issues of economic prosperity, democratic participation, and national leadership underpin the critiques of higher education put forth by such groups as the American Council on Education, the State Higher Education Executive Officers, and the Joint Committee for Review of the Master Plan for Higher Education of the California Legislature.[1] Equality of access, which permitted multicultural participation in higher education, is no longer enough. This goal has been replaced with that of parity of results, ensuring the successful participation in higher education by members of multicultural groups.

Goals and definitions of diversity in higher education have also undergone change. Levine traced the meaning of diversity through four sequential phases, all of which he stated are present on college and university campuses today. The first concept of diversity, with its roots in the 1960s, he called representation, with a focus on bringing more underrepresented populations to campus. The second notion of diversity, support, began in the 1970s and focused on sustaining these new students with a variety of services and programs. Integration was a third concept, with an emphasis on making the new populations part of the existing campus community, partly in reaction to the campus separatism of the 1980s. The fourth concept was multiculturalism, a development of the 1990s, which emphasized creating a shared community that maintains the integrity of the different groups composing it through such mechanisms as general education diversity requirements and orientation programs for majority students on diversity.[2]

Obstacles Faced by Multicultural Students

The problems challenging multicultural students are in some ways as diverse as the groups from which they come. Yet all of these students face several common barriers. Richardson and Skinner noted that students of color experience frustration when they are recruited by institutions on the strengths of their previous achievements and cultural affiliations but then are expected to become like Anglo students with whom they may have little in common. Their frustrations deepen as differences in preparation and learning preferences translate into often insurmountable barriers to education.[3]

Attrition and Attainment

For all multicultural groups, the issues of attrition and attainment are paramount. Early attrition is extremely high—even at the community college level, considered the most accessible point of entry for many multicultural students. This has been primarily attributed to inadequate high school preparation, insufficient financial support, stress, and alienation between multicultural students and their educational institutions.

Alienation is consistently identified as a persistent problem in every multicultural student group. Loo and Rolison studied alienation of multicultural students at a predominantly Anglo institution. They found that sociocultural alienation was pervasive and that it could be distinct from academic satisfaction for these students.[4] Thus, no matter how outstanding the academic achievement, multicultural students can feel alienated if their ethnic representation on campus is small. Alienation becomes a barrier to achievement for even academically successful multicultural students, undermining their ability to successfully matriculate and graduate.

Connection to the educational institution is a very important factor in overcoming this alienation and improving college persistence rates for all students.[5] In one study of multicultural student retention, Mallinckrodt and Sedlacek found that use of campus facilities was positively related to academic success and retention. The strongest relationship which they found was between African-American student retention and use of the undergraduate library.[6]

A Diversity of Barriers

As with many matters in race relations, the myriad of problems facing multicultural students from particular ethnic groups are obscured by stereotypical characterizations. However, the literature indicates several clusters of issues that can be associated generally with students from various backgrounds.

The cultural-deficit model often used to explain low performance by Hispanic students is intrinsically negative in its view of the impact of cultural values and the lack of emphasis on education.[7] However, Olivas asserted that the problem is far more complicated and entangled with the political disenfranchisement of Hispanics in American society.[8] Language proficiency, lack of study skills, cultural differences in time management, and the need for individualized communication and interaction are frequently cited as barriers which Hispanic students face.[9]

Many studies have been done contrasting the success of African-American students at predominantly white universities with their counterparts at historically black colleges and universities. A common theme in the research results was that African-American students have an increased tendency to suffer identity problems on Anglo campuses, subsequently interfering with their academic functioning.[10] Predictors of student success for African Americans that differed from those of Anglos including having instructors with non-traditional teaching styles and the feeling of being discriminated against on campus.[11] Study patterns for African-American students differ in that they are more likely to study alone and not seek aid from teaching assistants than students of some other ethnic backgrounds.[12]

The high attainment levels of some Asian-American students have engendered the label *model minority,* causing many people to overlook differences in communication style and learning patterns. The high use of study groups by Asian-American students has been shown to be helpful in insuring success in areas such as mathematics, but faculty have had difficulties attributing individual achievement in some classroom settings.[13] Bicultural dilemmas can emerge for these students as they attempt to balance learned cultural values of conformity, nonassertiveness, interdependence, and cooperation with behavioral expectations of assertion, independence and individualism found in American college classrooms.[14]

The deceptive umbrella term *Asian American* also does not reflect the diversity within this group. By 1980, the United States census counted six specific Asian ethnic groups: Chinese, Filipino, Japanese, Asian Indian, Korean, and Vietnamese,[15] each of which has further variety in terms of ancestry, language, culture, and economic status. In addition, the substantial needs of the recent Asian immigrant and refugee populations who are entering U.S. colleges in increasing numbers are often ignored as a result of the model-minority perceptions.[16] Language proficiency and differences in communication styles can often create barriers for some students.[17] Many of the obstacles created by cultural variations described above are quite pronounced for these students as well.[18]

The barriers for Native Americans, especially those from reservations, who are seeking college degrees are formidable: reservations are isolated, chronically neglected regions with persistent problems such as alcoholism and unemployment.[19] For some of these students, failure is viewed as the expectation, particularly in education, and building self-confidence is essential to success.[20] Maturity and life experiences off of the reservations are important predictors of success.[21] In addition, differences in cultural values between Anglo and tribal Native-American life can make it difficult for some students to be successful in an educational system based on Anglo values and behaviors.[22]

Changing Institutional Perspectives

A study of the recent literature on barriers to multicultural achievement in higher education makes it clear that the complexity of the issues involved demands a perspective that considers how colleges and universities are failing to meet the needs of multicultural students, rather than one which concentrates on why multicultural students are failing to perform in these institutions. As Thoeny pointed out, the easy gains in the first wave of multicultural enrollment in predominantly Anglo institutions have passed, and higher education is now faced with the prospect of attracting and qualifying multicultural students with less academic preparation and family support than those who have made up the first 10 percent of the progress in this area.[23] Continued advancement in recruiting and retaining multicultural students will require significant change in institutional goals, missions, and values.

Models of successful organizational change in support of cultural diversity, though few in number, do exist.[24] A good summary of the fundamental issues of organizing universities to respond to cultural diversity appeared in a recent report by Smith who identified these areas for change: diversity of faculty and staff, statements of mission and values, programs of comprehensive education for diversity, methods for dealing with conflict, focus on the quality of interaction, and mediation of the perceived conflict between quality and diversity.[25] De los Santos and Richardson identified these institutional practices for removing race and ethnicity as factors in college completion: publicly stated priorities, commitment of discretionary dollars to recruitment and retention of multicultural students, visible multicultural leadership, good data, a systematic and coordinated approach to meeting student needs, an uncompromising emphasis on quality which accommodates diversity, strong collaboration with public schools, other colleges and community agencies, a supportive learning environment, a high value on diversity among the faculty, a rewards system for good teaching, and perception of "comfortability" in the social environment.[26]

The Multicultural Transformation

Significant change in culture is necessary for the transformation to a multicultural organization. Bensimon and Tierney defined multiculturalism as

> a complex set of relationships framed around issues of race, gender, class, sexual orientation, and power. One of the struggles in multicultural organizations is to understand the commonalities and differences among underrepresented groups, and to develop an appreciation of how an understanding of these characteristics might create alliances for change.[27]

They went on to say that to create multicultural campuses, a model needs to be envisioned that is not organized along patriarchal, white, heterosexual norms. The institution and its organizational culture need to change in the areas of people, mission, structure, and curriculum.[28]

As colleges and universities move beyond the assimilation model to approaches based on mutual respect and celebration of differences, decisions involving fundamental perspectives about community, learning, teaching, and resource allocation will be questioned and changed. Campuses will need to learn from the inevitable conflict emerging from this shift in paradigm to find the balance between fragmentation and homogeneity in ways which promote multicultural perspectives.[29]

In a study of ten institutions with high levels of success in multicultural-student graduation, Richardson and Skinner identified the tensions between diversity and quality, and the processes through which institutions adapt to resolve these tensions, as central to the understanding of this success. Their basic premise was that, as faculty and staff adapt their behaviors to respond to initiatives from campus administration, the organizational culture will shift to provide a more productive academic and social environment for students who differ in preparation or culture from those an institution has traditionally served.[30]

Richardson and Skinner presented a comprehensive model of this institutional adaptation to student diversity consisting of three stages:

1. the reactive stage, where the emphasis is on increasing participation rates through interventions related to recruiting, financial aid, and admissions;
2. the strategic stage, characterized by longer-term outreach and collaboration strategies to expand the pool of prepared multicultural applicants and programs to ease the transition for entering students who differ in preparation, objectives, or background from those traditionally served; and
3. the adaptive stage, where interventions in student assessment, learning assistance, pedagogy, and curriculum content are addressed from a multicultural perspective according to student need rather than race or ethnicity. Unlike the earlier two stages,

in the adaptive stage, institutions value their multicultural status
as a strength rather than seeing diversity as a threat to quality.[31]

The concepts that form the basis of this model are
beginning to permeate college and university campuses in
ways which suggest institutional change, at least in terms
of the curriculum. In a study of 196 colleges and universities representative of American higher education, Levine
and Cureton found that 34 percent had a multicultural
general education requirement, at least 33 percent offered
coursework in ethnic and gender studies, and 54 percent
had introduced multiculturalism into departmental offerings,
primarily by adding new material to existing courses. A
majority of the campuses were seeking to increase faculty
diversity, and 72 percent of the vice presidents and deans
surveyed stated that multiculturalism was a major issue
which they dealt with continually.[32]

The question of how this growing campus emphasis on
diversity is affecting students was addressed in a recent
empirical study which compared the status of 25,000
entering college freshmen in the fall of 1985 with their
situations four years later in 1989. In an analysis of eighty-
two outcome measures on these students, Astin found that
emphasizing diversity either as a matter of institutional
policy or in faculty research and teaching, as well as
providing students with curricular and extracurricular
opportunities to confront racial and multicultural issues, are
all associated with widespread beneficial effects on a
student's cognitive and affective development.[33]

The Library's Role in Diversity

The issues raised in the higher education literature on
cultural diversity deserve serious consideration in academic

libraries for several reasons. If our institutions are going to change, then our libraries may need to change with them. These models for adapting to diversity suggest that to be part of this adaptation, librarians may need to rethink assumptions about students, faculty, curriculum, and pedagogy.

As part of larger institutions facing changing student bodies, librarians may find it useful to develop an understanding of where their universities are in adapting to the changing student population. The three-stage model of institutional adaptation described by Richardson and Skinner offers one framework for examining these issues. The strategic stage, with its emphasis on transitional support services, suggests one role for the library; the adaptive stage, moving into issues of learning assistance, curricular content, and pedagogical change, suggests other areas for library involvement.

The emphasis on support services in the models for successful campus diversity, particularly those in the academic arena, offer the library important opportunities for becoming directly involved. In developing library services which are responsive to the needs of multicultural as well as Anglo students, a number of questions need to be considered:

- What relevance does the research on alienation and other barriers to success cited above have for libraries?
- In creating a supportive learning environment for all students, how can issues of differing study patterns, communication modes, learning styles, and language proficiencies be addressed?
- Should programs and services which have been developed, perhaps unconsciously, with the needs of

dominant-culture students in mind, be reconsidered, taking into account varying multicultural perspectives?

- How can the perception among multicultural students that the library is an important and accessible component of their education be promoted?

Notes

1. American Council on Education, *One-Third of a Nation; a Report of the Commission on Minority Participation in Education and American Life* (Washington, DC: American Council on Education and Education Commission of the States, 1988); California, Legislature, Joint Committee for Review of the Master Plan for Higher Education, *California Faces... California's Future; Education for Citizenship in a Multicultural Democracy* (Sacramento, CA: Joint Legislative Publications Office, 1989); and State Higher Education Executive Officers, *A Difference of Degrees: State Initiatives to Improve Minority Student Achievement* (Denver, CO: State Higher Education Executive Officers, 1987).

2. Arthur Levine, "The Meaning of Diversity," *Change* 23 (1991): 4-5.

3. Richard C. Richardson and Elizabeth Fisk Skinner, *Achieving Quality and Diversity; Universities in a Multicultural Society* (New York: Macmillan, 1991), 11.

4. Chalsa Loo and Garry Rolison, "Alienation of Ethnic Minority Students at a Predominantly White University," *Journal of Higher Education* 57 (1986): 58-77.

5. Vincent Tinto, *Leaving College; Rethinking the Causes and Cures of Student Attrition* (Chicago, IL: University of Chicago Press, 1987).

6. Brent Mallinckrodt and William F. Sedlacek, "Student Retention and the Use of Campus Facilities by Race," *NASPA Journal* 24 (1987): 28-32.

7. Teresa McKenna and Flora Ida Ortiz, eds. *The Broken Web: The Educational Experience of Hispanic American Women* (Berkeley, CA: The Tomas Rivera Center and Floricanto Press, 1988), 7.

8. Michael A. Olivas, ed. *Latino College Students* (New York: Teachers College Press, 1986), 1, 13.

9. Raymond V. Padilla, "Assessing Heuristic Knowledge to Enhance College Students' Success," in *Assessment and Access; Hispanics in Higher Education*, ed. Gary D. Keller, James R. Deneen, and Raphael J. Magallan (Albany: State University of New York Press, 1991), 86-91; Maria Magdalena Llabre, "Time as a Factor in the Cognitive Test Performance of Latino College Students," in *Assessment and Access; Hispanics in Higher Education*, ed. Gary D. Keller, James R. Deneen, and Raphael J. Magallan (Albany: State University of New York Press, 1991), 95-104; and Olivas, 5.

10. Jacqueline Fleming, *Blacks in College* (San Francisco: Jossey-Bass, 1985), 21-22; and Walter R. Allen, "The Color of Success: African-American College Student Outcomes at Predominantly White and Historically Black Public Colleges and Universities," *Harvard Educational Review* 62 (1992): 26-44.

11. Michael T. Nettles, "Racial Similarities and Differences in the Predictors of College Student Attainment," in *College in Black and White*, ed. Walter R. Allen, Edgar G. Epps and Nesha Z. Haniff (Albany: State University of New York Press, 1991), 81.

12. Robert E. Fullilove and Philip Uri Treisman, "Mathematics Achievement Among African American Undergraduates at the University of California, Berkeley: An Evaluation of the Mathematics Workshop Program," *Journal of Negro Education* 59 (1990): 466.

13. Fullilove and Treisman, 468.

14. Maurianne Adams, "Cultural Inclusion in the American College Classroom," *New Directions for Teaching and Learning* no. 49 (1992): 7.

15. Jayjia Hsia and Marsha Hirano-Nakanishi, "The Demographics of Diversity: Asian Americans and Higher Education," *Change* 21 (1989): 23.

16. Jayjia Hsia, *Asian Americans in Higher Education and at Work* (New Jersey: Lawrence Erlbaum Associates, 1988), 18; and Bob H. Suzuki, "Asian Americans as the 'Model Minority,'" *Change* 21 (1989): 14.

17. Suzuki, 18.

18. Adams, 7.

19. Carnegie Foundation for the Advancement of Teaching, "Native Americans and Higher Education: New Mood of Optimism," *Change* 22 (1990): 29.

20. Ernest L. Boyer, *Tribal Colleges; Shaping the Future of Native America* (Lawrenceville, NJ: Carnegie Foundation for the Advancement of Teaching, 1989), 3.

21. Norman T. Oppelt, *The Tribally Controlled Indian College; The Beginnings of Self Determination in American Indian Education* (Tsaile, AZ: Navajo Community College Press, 1990), 80.

22. Norman T. Oppelt, "Cultural Values and Behaviors Common Among Tribal American Indians: A Resource for Student Service Administrators," *NASPA Journal* 26 (1989): 167-179.

23. A. Robert Thoeny, "Strategies for Action," in *Toward Black Undergraduate Student Equality in American Higher Education*, ed. Michael T. Nettles (Westport, CT: Greenwood Press, 1988), 198.

24. Gale S. Auletta and Terry Jones, "Reconstituting the Inner Circle," *American Behavioral Scientist* 34 (1990): 137-152; and Cynthia Woolbright, ed. *Valuing Diversity on Campus: A Multicultural Approach* (Bloomington, IN: Association of College Unions-International, 1989).

25. Daryl G. Smith, *The Challenge of Diversity: Involvement or Alienation in the Academy?* Report No.5. (Washington, DC: School of Education and Human Development, George Washington University, 1989), 45-67.

26. Alfredo de los Santos and Richard C. Richardson, "Ten Principles for Good Institution Practice in Removing Race/Ethnicity as a Factor in College Completion," *Educational Record* 69 (1988): 43-46.

27. Estela M. Bensimon and William G. Tierney, "Shaping the Multicultural Campus; Strategies for Administrators," *College Board Review* 166 (1992/93): 5.

28. Ibid., 6.

29. Daryl G. Smith, "Embracing Diversity as a Central Campus Goal," *Academe* 76 (1990): 31.

30. Richardson and Skinner, 11.

31. Ibid., 11-14.

32. Arthur Levine and Jeanette Cureton, "The Quiet Revolution; Eleven Facts About Multiculturalism and the Curriculum," *Change* 24 (1992): 25-29.

33. Alexander W. Astin, "Diversity and Multiculturalism on the Campus; How Are Students Affected?" *Change* 25 (1993): 44-49.

3
ACADEMIC LIBRARIES
AND MULTICULTURAL STUDENTS

Overview

As student populations have changed at colleges and universities across the country, some academic librarians have begun to examine the means by which they provide library services and support, exploring new alternatives for their development. The impetus for these considerations is clear. As Trujillo and Weber pointed out:

> Many U.S. faculty, students, and professional library staff—especially those from minority ethnic and racial groups—recognize that American academic libraries are failing in significant ways. They would argue that several conditions are still far from being acceptable: library staff diversity is insufficient (particularly at the professional and administrative levels); information services for minority communities are not readily available or effective; and the current organizational environment does not support or encourage library-wide staff development and advancement or campus-wide service improvement.[1]

Some libraries have come to understand that their long-term future as institutions may be linked to the development of programs and resources that meet the needs of culturally diverse patrons.[2] Visions of the future which include active roles for libraries on pluralistic campuses emphasize the need for change in such areas as leadership, recruitment, communication, sensitivity, marketing, collections, outreach, and priorities.[3] As librarians confront these challenges, a growing body of literature has emerged providing program examples for many parts of this vision.

Public Libraries

The library service response to changing demographics took place first at the public library level, where changes in the community had a direct impact upon public service. This response is well documented in the professional library literature beginning in the late 1960s. Wertheimer's special issue of *Library Trends* captured this literature well, providing an overview of services and programs in settings around the world.[4] More recently, Quezada outlined effective approaches to multicultural community library needs in professional library organizations, state and federal agencies, and major public libraries.[5]

Two research projects on the significance for public libraries of the growing ethnic and racial diversity in the state of California are of particular interest for their implications for academic libraries. After developing a profile of public libraries and of racial and ethnic demographics for the state, Payne considered systematic obstacles which libraries face when responding to diversity and made recommendations for actions to facilitate change.[6] It is interesting to note that Payne found librarians' concerns regarding the disparity between library users and the population to be strong and continuing but found little evidence that elected officials or multicultural group leaders were concerned with the level of library services being provided to multicultural communities. In a published reaction to this study, characterized as a *minority report*, Tarin took Payne to task for describing barriers to service in terms of inadequacies on the part of the ethnic person rather than in terms of inadequacies in the libraries' services.[7]

The Center for Policy Development was not as positive in its assessment of California's libraries and librarians, raising serious questions about the capacity and willingness of these public libraries to serve the increasingly diverse communities of the state. The few examples of effective services identified in this study were marked by systematic programs to assess multicultural patrons' information needs, efforts to change attitudes and behaviors of persons inside and outside the libraries, and vigorous library leadership that was willing to take the steps needed to assure continuing quality services to all of the community's residents.[8]

Academic Libraries

The literature on academic library services to multicultural students is more recent. With the exception of one newsletter item,[9] the focus of related articles in the early and mid-1980s was on the services to international students (see Chapter 4).

Substantive reports of academic library programs and services to multicultural students in academic libraries first appeared in the literature in 1988. One leader in this field has been the University of Michigan. In its 1988 report, *Point of Intersection: The University Library and the Pluralistic Campus Community*, Michigan defined the role of the library this way:

By its very nature as a haven for diverse collections and ideas
and as a facility that necessarily attracts a diverse staff and
academic population, the Library recognizes its role as a primary
point of intersection for the vast numbers of peoples and interests
that exist on the campus. Intrinsic to its professional mission,
then, is its encouragement of an understanding of pluralism as
both fact and ideal in the academic world and beyond.[10]

This vision is carried out at Michigan in programs of staff
training to improve sensitivity to cultural diversity, peer
counseling for library skills, library instruction techniques
aimed at improving multicultural student achievement, and
outreach to identify needs and build relationships.[11]

Multicultural Student Needs

Inherent in the development of services for multicultural
student populations is the recognition that their needs vary
from those of the dominant-culture students for whom most
academic library programs have been designed. Multicultural student needs for library services have been described
in the literature in several ways, primarily related to
student contact through library public services and to the
librarian's role in providing library instruction.

The importance of library skills in student success is the
basis for these perspectives. Understanding what students
seek and need from education provides librarians as well as
other educators with the background to offer instruction
and services in the manner best suited to each student.[12]
An awareness of the general cultural and linguistic values
of diverse populations is viewed as an essential tool for
educators that makes possible more effective communication while avoiding potential conflicts and establishing an
atmosphere that will facilitate learning.[13] An understand-

- Intercultural communication skills—the ability to send and interpret verbal and nonverbal messages accurately in different cultures;
- Gear-shifting—the ability to re-adjust expectations, modify plans, try out new approaches, and rebound from setbacks; and
- Intercultural facilitation skills—the ability to manage cultural differences and use these differences to the operations' benefit.[21]

In essence, the goal is to train people in what Green calls *ethnic competence*: "the ability to conduct one's work in a way that is congruent with the behavior and expectations that members of a distinctive culture recognize as appropriate among themselves."[22] Huston put this into a compelling framework for librarians, stating:

- Where we stand affects what we see, what we look for, and where we look. These factors, in turn, affect what we find.
- Information consists of observations about the world that are affected by the contexts in which observations are made.
- Information is valuable only in relation to the context in which it is used. In other words, information is situationally based and changes meaning according to context.
- The receiver of the message participates actively in determining meaning.
- The meaning that is created depends upon previously learned cultural codes, life experience, the present situation, and individual perspectives, all of which serve as filters through which a message is subjected.
- The ultimate test of the value of an information service is the helpfulness of the information to the user in terms of what he or she is trying to do or know at a particular moment in space and time.[23]

As recent incidences of violence in law enforcement agencies across the country have demonstrated, behaviors of those on the front lines are crucial to the overall responsiveness of public service agencies to multicultural populations. Training may not be able to change personal attitudes, but it can attempt to change official behavior. The above-mentioned programs as well as information from the Association of Research Libraries[24] provide good models for academic libraries in training for multicultural sensitivity. Resources may also be available within local campus faculties and communities, since the business, education, and social service sectors are far ahead of libraries in acknowledging the need for such training programs.

Implications for Bibliographic Instruction

Library instruction is also being reevaluated in light of our increasingly diverse student populations. During the last decade, the shift to online public catalogs and the proliferation of end-user database tools have made effective bibliographic instruction even more important, because without the ability to negotiate these systems, library users will increasingly be at a general disadvantage in their ability to access information.[25] Today's environment poses challenges for library instruction, for often a single presentation must be effective for groups of markedly diverse students. As Wilson pointed out:

> Diversity in learners is nothing new in libraries, but it seems that librarians only recently have acknowledged and responded to learners as a heterogeneous population. Too often library instruction programs have been designed with the generic student in mind.[26]

Much research in the educational field shows that cognitive style, learning style, and culture are interrelated. Dunn asserted that although each of the ethnic and racial groups involved in this research includes individuals with widely diversified learning styles, within certain populations statistically more individuals used the same or a similar cluster of specific techniques to gain knowledge, distinguishing their methods from those of other populations.[27] In particular, Singh found that members of Mexican and Asian cultures tend to have field-dependent cognitive styles, but the principal teaching style found in western higher education is based on field-independent learning, which assumes that the student is likely to perceive items as discrete from the organized whole. He argued that to be effective, teachers need to recognize the range of cognitive and learning styles among their students.[28]

In a study of instruction for sixty-five culturally diverse adult learners inexperienced in library research, Huston found that a network model which made students an active part of the educational process was an effective technique for inclusive instruction. The students' initial points of reference and conceptual frameworks formed the starting point for the teaching session. A curriculum design based upon knowledge of the users and their collective strengths rather than on the librarians' professional strengths was found to be beneficial in reaching culturally diverse users.[29]

Fink incorporated an approach she calls *diverse thinking* into her bibliographic instruction sessions. This approach takes into account the varied learning styles of students from different backgrounds and suggests that a variety of teaching approaches may be necessary to reach everyone. Diverse thinking also involves identifying alternative perspectives and applying conceptual technologies to push the boundaries of one's own thinking. In bibliographic instruction, diverse thinking pushes the boundaries of the library, library skills, acceptable information, and even one's comfort zones. Her pedagogy utilizes a variety of teaching techniques for creative problem solving and critical thinking. For example, brainstorming and clustering are added to more traditional analytical approaches to problem solving. Most important is the concept of alternative approaches to the material being presented, in order to effectively reach as many students as possible.[30]

In developing a pedagogy which is sensitive to cultural diversity, Hall asserted that the importance lies not so much with teaching style or content, but with "intangible qualities of personal rapport and empathy [which] play a vital role within the pedagogical paradigm."[31] In working with students of color, what Hall called *affectivity*, the relationships developed between teacher and student inside and outside the classroom, is one of the most important factors in making the connections which promote learning. In addition to importance for bibliographic instruction in the classroom, these concepts are valuable in considering effective reference desk interaction between librarians and diverse users.

Within the broader context of library instruction programs, one innovative approach to reaching multicultural students has been the development of peer counseling programs for library skills. One such program at the University of Michigan's Undergraduate Library, built upon the long-recognized fact that many students turn first to their peers for advice and help, recruits and trains multicultural students to assist undergraduates of all backgrounds to use the resources of the library. These student counselors provide individual assistance in using electronic resources, doing basic research and simple reference, developing term paper topics, and acting as guides to the various libraries on campus. In addition to providing an innovative way to support undergraduates in their use of the library, this program creates positive multicultural role models for all students by exposing them to highly competent peers in positions of responsibility.[32]

Another program at the University of Michigan addresses the issue of student preparation levels in advance of entrance to college. Acknowledging the serious need for improving the library skills of incoming first-year students, especially those who are from underrepresented multicultural groups, reference librarians work with high school librarians and the campus minority outreach office to provide special library instruction resources for selected Michigan high school students.[33]

Diversity Positions

Several models exist for the development of a librarian position with responsibility for multicultural services. At the University of Michigan, the position of Diversity Librarian was established in 1988 to provide assistance to multicultural graduate students and faculty in their areas of research and teaching, support research and instruction in the areas of gender, race and ethnic studies, further departmental and administrative diversity initiatives, and monitor and coordinate library acquisitions in the areas of gender, race and ethnic studies.[34]

The University of California, Santa Cruz, developed their position of Multicultural Services Librarian in 1988, using an outreach services model borrowed from public libraries. Public libraries have extensive outreach programs developed by librarians who have the ability to communicate with, gain the trust of, and inspire those who are not reached by traditional library services, and then to tailor services to meet the needs of these people. Recognizing the potential value of these outreach skills for use with multicultural students in the university environment, the University of California, Santa Cruz, hired a children's librarian from an urban public library to serve as their first multicultural services librarian. This librarian was charged with providing leadership in library services for the campus multicultural community, developing and coordinating outreach programs, and providing library instruction and specialized reference services in multicultural studies.[35]

Positions combining various aspects from these two models also exist at Stanford University[36] and at several other ARL libraries.[37]

Collections

Expanding curricula and diverse interests require the availability of information resources needed to support teaching and research from a pluralistic and global point of view.[38] In addition, academic library programs serving multicultural students have begun to include resources that are relevant to and reflective of these students' cultural backgrounds.[39] According to E.J. Josey, "students from the various ethnic groups will be encouraged to read books about their history, literature, leaders and folk heroes if academic libraries purchase books in these subject areas and then make them available."[40]

Although all collection development programs may not have formal provisions for acquiring these materials, many are making efforts to select more than the major trade and university press publications. Active efforts still are necessary to learn where multicultural scholars are publishing, how the standards of ethnic studies are developing, and what the impact is on other disciplines such as history and sociology. Enhanced access to a broad spectrum of opinions, to a new history, to a new view of lost history has become a necessity at many institutions.

One useful tool in identifying these information sources is entitled *Developing Library Collections for California's Emerging Majority; A Manual of Resources for Ethnic Collection Development*.[41] Although this is obviously geared to the west coast, it contains many helpful leads to non-traditional publishing sources for ethnic and cultural materials. A recent study of ethnic collection development activities among City University of New York libraries indicated that in addition to traditional selection tools, the most useful approaches to collection development in this area were regular visits to ethnic bookstores and collaboration with colleagues in ethnic studies disciplines.[42] An important new journal from Greenwood Press, *Multi-Cultural Review*, provides subjective reviews of print and non-print multicultural materials and information on the subject of multiculturalism.

Another critical issue in the area of collection development for cultural diversity is bibliographic control. Access to much of this literature, particularly the primary source documents pertaining to ethnic and racial groups, can be quite difficult. Material is often scattered, and approaches need to be creative and cross many discipline lines. Often multicultural students may assume that a library's holdings in their areas of interest are inadequate, when they are actually available but difficult to identify. Eventually this may mean changing our approach to classification and indexing. For example, Library of Congress subject headings are not always reflective of works based on non-traditional perspectives or relevant to those seeking ethnic literature.[43]

A strong collection development policy has been shown to be one of the most important tools in supporting the growth of multicultural collections. Specific budget strategies and specially identified funds can also be important factors in these endeavors. Well-developed and -publicized collections of materials related to the backgrounds of various multicultural groups on campus have proven to be effective drawing cards to bring students into the library and lead them to other services.[44] Exhibits of library holdings have been developed to make these resources more visible while adding a pluralistic dimension to the cultural contributions of the library to campus life.

Recruitment and Education

The recruitment of people of color into library careers has long been an important goal of the profession.[45] Issues of affirmative action and representation as well as effective and responsive library programs for multicultural populations form the basis for this goal. As Koyama, frequent speaker on multiculturalism in libraries has said, "If we do not want a South African environment in our libraries, we must diversify at administrative and faculty levels, not just among the staff and student assistants."[46] The shift in priorities in academic library programs and resources described above also presents challenges for library educators. As new skills have become needed for librarians functioning in a diverse environment, the profession itself finds that it needs to become more diverse.

Although the enrollment of multicultural students in graduate and professional schools has increased substantially over the last decade,[47] the number of multicultural students receiving masters degrees from accredited library programs has declined.[48] This has been a growing concern in academic libraries, resulting in the active involvement of many librarians in efforts such as internships, fellowships, and institutional recruitment programs.[49] For example, the University of Delaware at Newark and the University of California, Santa Barbara, have full-time internships for recent library school graduates from underrepresented groups, providing professional experience in large academic libraries.[50] Such programs help to develop multicultural candidates for positions requiring previous experience.

The need for change also shows itself in library and information science education. Multiculturalism has become important in library school curricula not only to attract more people of color but also to ensure that all newly educated librarians have the knowledge and skills necessary to function effectively in a multicultural environment. Considerable work has begun to identify skills and propose specific curricular programs and activities to address these needs,[51] but much remains to be done in achieving this goal.

Notes

1. Roberto G. Trujillo and David C. Weber, "Academic Library Responses to Cultural Diversity: A Position Paper for the 1990s," *Journal of Academic Librarianship* 17 (1991): 158.

2. Rhonda Rios Kravitz, Adelia Lines, and Vivian Sykes, "Serving the Emerging Majority: Documenting Their Voices," *Library Administration and Management* 5 (1991): 184-188.

3. Janet E. Welch and R. Errol Lam, "The Library and the Pluralistic Campus in the Year 2000: Implications for Administrators," *Library Administration and Management* 5 (1991): 212-216; Cliff Glaviano and R. Errol Lam, "Academic Libraries and Affirmative Action: Approaching Cultural Diversity in the 1990s," *College and Research Libraries* 51 (1990): 513-523; Trujillo and Weber, 157-161; and Kravitz, Lines, and Sykes, 184-188.

4. M. Leonard Wertheimer, ed. "Library Services to Ethnocultural Minorities," *Library Trends* 29 (1980): 175-273.

5. Shelley Quezada, "Mainstreaming Library Services to Multicultural Populations: The Evolving Tapestry," *Wilson Library Bulletin* 66 (1992): 28-29, 120.

6. Judith Payne, *Public Libraries Face California's Ethnic and Racial Diversity* (Santa Monica, CA: RAND Corporation, 1988).

7. Patricia Tarin, "RAND Misses the Point: A Minority Report," *Library Journal* 113 (1988): 32.

8. Center for Policy Development, *Adrift in a Sea of Change; California's Public Libraries Struggle to Meet the Information Needs of Multicultural Communities* (Sacramento, CA: California State Library, 1990).

9. Linda J. Piele and Brian Yamel, "Reference Assistance Project at the University of Wisconsin-Parkside," *College and Research Libraries News* 43 (1982): 83-84.

10. University of Michigan Library, *Point of Intersection: The University Library and the Pluralistic Campus Community* (Ann Arbor, MI: The University of Michigan Library, 1988), 1.

11. Carla Stoffle, "A New Library for the New Undergraduate," *Library Journal* 115 (1990): 47-51; University of Michigan Library, *Point of Intersection: The University Library and the Pluralistic Campus Community* and *Point of Intersection II: The University Library Moves Toward Diversity* (Ann Arbor, MI: The University of Michigan Library, 1988 and 1990).

12. Welch and Lam, 213.

13. Li-Rong Lilly Cheng, "Recognizing Diversity; A Need for a Paradigm Shift," *American Behavioral Scientist* 34 (1990) 264.

14. Daniel Liestman, "The Disadvantaged Minority Student and the Academic Library," *Urban Academic Librarian* 8 (1991/1992): 13-19.

15. Paul Resta, "Organizing Education for Minorities: Enhancing Minority Access and Use of the New Information Technologies in Higher Education," *Education and Computing* 8 (1992): 119-127.

16. Kravitz, Lines, and Sykes, 185.

17. R. Errol Lam, "The Reference Interview: Some Intercultural Considerations," *RQ* 27 (1988): 390-395; Teresa B. Mensching, *Reaching and Teaching Diverse Library User Groups* (Ann Arbor, MI: Pierian Press, 1989); Phoebe Janes and Ellen Meltzer, "Origins and Attitudes: Training Reference Librarians for a Pluralistic World," *Reference Librarian* no. 30 (1990): 145-155; Patrick A. Hall, "Peanuts: A Note on Intercultural Communication," *Journal of Academic Librarianship* 18 (1992): 211-213; and Association of Research Libraries, Office of Management Studies, *Cultural Diversity Programming in ARL Libraries*, SPEC Kit #165 (Washington, DC: Association of Research Libraries, 1990).

18. Vivian Sykes, "Reference Service to the Multicultural Library User," *CARL Newsletter* 12 (1988): 2-3.

19. Janes and Meltzer, 148.

20. Louise Greenfield, Susan Johnston, and Karen Williams, "Educating the World: Training Library Staff to Communicate Effectively with International Students," *Journal of Academic Librarianship* 12 (1986): 227-231; Stoffle, 47-51; and Association of Research Libraries, Office of Management Studies, 105-163.

21. Janes and Meltzer, 148-149.

22. James Green, *Cultural Awareness in the Human Services* (Englewood Cliffs, NJ: Prentice-Hall, 1982), 53-59.

23. Mary M. Huston, "Building New Relationships and Valuing Diversity Through the Information Seeking Process: From Picture Books to Hyper Space," *MultiCultural Review* 1 (1992): 13.

24. Association of Research Libraries, Office of Management Studies, 105-163.

25. Mary M. Huston, "May I Introduce You: Teaching Culturally Diverse End-Users Through Everyday Information Seeking Experiences," *Reference Services Review* 17 (1989): 7.

26. Lizabeth A. Wilson, "Changing Users: Bibliographic Instruction for Whom?" in *The Evolving Educational Mission of the Library* ed. Betsy Baker and Mary Ellen Litzinger (Chicago: Association of College and Research Libraries, 1992), 20-53.

27. Rita Dunn, "Learning Styles of the Multiculturally Diverse," *Emergency Librarian* 20 (1993): 24-32.

28. B.R. Singh, "Cognitive Styles, Cultural Pluralism and Effective Teaching and Learning," *International Review of Education* 34 (1988): 355-370.

29. Huston, "May I Introduce You," 7-11.

30. Deborah Fink, "Diverse Thinking: Pushing the Boundaries of Bibliographic Instruction" (paper presented at the Association of College and Research Libraries' preconference, *Cultural Diversity and Higher Education*, Atlanta, GA, 28 June 1991).

31. Patrick A. Hall, "The Role of Affectivity in Instructing People of Color: Some Implications for Bibliographic Instruction," *Library Trends* 39 (1991): 316-326.

32. Barbara MacAdam and Darlene P. Nichols, "Peer Information Counseling: An Academic Library Program for Minority Students," *Journal of Academic Librarianship* 15 (1989): 204-209; Stoffle, 47-51.

33. Patricia A. Tarin, "The Good, the Undergrad, and the UGLi," *Library Journal* 115 (1990): 51.

34. University of Michigan Library, *Point of Intersection II*, 14.

35. Allan J. Dyson, "Reaching Out for Outreach; A University Library Develops a New Position to Serve the School's Multicultural Students," *American Libraries* 20 (1989): 952-954.

36. Association of Research Libraries, Office of Management Studies, 185-188.

37. Otis A. Chadley, "Addressing Cultural Diversity in Academic and Research Libraries," *College and Research Libraries* 53 (1992): 210.

38. Trujillo and Weber, 160.

39. James A. Hefner and Lelia G. Rhodes, "Excellence in Education: Libraries Facilitating Learning for Minority Students," in *Libraries and the Search for Academic Excellence*, ed. Patricia Senn Breivik and Robert Wedgeworth (Metuchen NJ: Scarecrow Press, 1988), 66.

40. E. J. Josey, "The Role of the Academic Library in Serving the Disadvantaged Student," *Library Trends* 20 (1971): 439.

41. Katharine T. A. Scarborough, ed. *Developing Library Collections for California's Emerging Majority* (Berkeley, CA: Bay Area Library and Information System and the School of Library and Information Studies, University of California, Berkeley, 1990).

42. Claudia J. Gollop, "Selection and Acquisition of Multicultural Materials at the Libraries of the City University of New York," *Urban Academic Librarian* 8 (1991/1992): 20-29.

43. Katharine T. A. Scarborough, "Collections for the Emerging Majority," *Library Journal* 116 (1991): 44-47.

44. Ibid.

45. Lois Buttlar and William Caynon, "Recruitment of Librarians into the Profession: The Minority Perspective," *Library and Information Science Research* 14 (1992): 259; and Kristin H. Gerhard and Jeanne M.K. Boydston, "A Library Committee on Diversity and Its Role in a Library Diversity Program," *College and Research Libraries* 54 (1993): 335-343.

46. Janice Koyama, "Multiculturalism, Money, and 'Where's the Meat?'" (Paper presented at the Association of College and Research Libraries' preconference, *Cultural Diversity and Higher Education*, Atlanta, GA, 28 June 1991).

47. Lorene Brown, "Student Admission and Multicultural Recruitment," *Journal of Library Administration* 16 (1992): 109.

48. Ibid., 110; and E.J. Josey, "Education for Library Services to Cultural Minorities," *Journal of Multicultural Librarianship* 5 (1991): 104-111.

49. Joyce C. Wright, "Recruitment and Retention of Minorities in Academic Libraries: A Plan for Action for the 1990s," *Illinois Libraries* 72 (1990): 621-625; Association of Research Libraries, Office of Management Studies, *Minority Recruitment and Retention in ARL Libraries*, SPEC Kit #167 (Washington, DC: Association of Research Libraries, 1990); and Kay F. Jones, "Multicultural Diversity and the Academic Library," *Urban Academic Librarian* 8 (1990/1991): 14-22.

50. "Delaware Establishes Affirmative Action Internship," *Wilson Library Bulletin* 59 (1984):170-171; and Joseph A. Boissé and Connie V. Dowell, "Increasing Minority Librarians in Academic Research Libraries," *Library Journal* 112 (1987): 52-54.

51. Susan J. Freiband, "Multicultural Issues and Concerns in Library Education," *Journal of Library and Information Science* 33 (1992): 287-294.

4
INTERNATIONAL STUDENTS
IN AMERICAN LIBRARIES

Introduction

International students comprise one segment of the student population which already has been recognized by American librarians as having distinctive needs and requiring special services. The increasing presence of international students on American campuses has become a phenomenon which most librarians take for granted, and orientation and bibliographic instruction designed specifically for these students have become well established in many libraries' programs.[1]

The significant growth in the populations of international students enrolled in colleges and universities in the United States, which has increased over one-hundredfold since World War II,[2] led to a myriad of articles in the library literature in the 1980s describing problems, techniques, and programs related to these students. While there is something to be learned from this literature in considering how library services based on the dominant culture need modification for effective use by others—two authors go so far as to say that "a parallel can be drawn between foreign students and disadvantaged students from this country"[3]—there are distinctions between international students and multicultural students, defined here as being American, which must be kept in mind when reviewing this work.

Most important is the explicit understanding in most institutions of higher education that international students bring with them the need for an initial period of adjustment and orientation, specialized institutional support and, at the individual level, additional effort in communication. These needs are met with highly developed support programs, particularly on campuses where more than 5 percent of the student body is international.[4] In addition, many students come from backgrounds of considerable privilege and are well supported through financial incentives from their governments.

Yet some of this experience in academic libraries is worth noting here, particularly in the areas of cultural sensitivity, communication skills, and training programs. The shift in perspective necessary to understand the needs of international students confronting academic libraries is particularly salient. Moorhead described the assumptions underlying library programs in this way:

> Growing up in any academic environment, even in a society as multinational and diverse as the United States, we emerge with a set of perceptions that are strikingly similar and largely unrecognized by ourselves as peculiar to us. Our shared commonalities are seen best when they are not shared, or when they become uncommon.[5]

If one interprets this not only in the international context in which it was written but expands it to include the distinctions between dominant-culture librarians and multicultural students, the basis for building upon this work may be seen.

resources for their new classmates through peer assistance programs at several universities.[12]

Collaborative relationships with English as a Second Language programs have also provided good opportunities for library instruction. Cornell University has had a longstanding program which includes active involvement for librarians in a guided research project which gives students the experience of working through their own individually assigned topics. Librarians then participate in class discussions of these projects, using openings to clarify misunderstandings and reinforce important principles.[13] Augsburg College, the University of Arizona, and Roosevelt University have also reported on successful programs integrated with English language instruction.[14]

Teaching Techniques

Teaching methods need to be adjusted for the varied audiences which groups of international students constitute. A simplified approach to concepts, use of concrete examples, and hands-on practice are basic principles of bibliographic instruction which become even more important in this setting. Greenfield, Johnston, and Williams offered these specific pointers for library instructors:

- Avoid using complex sentence structure and vocabulary.
- Define and repeat important words or concepts. Use synonyms for difficult words to help explain their meanings.
- Avoid using library jargon unless absolutely necessary.
- Avoid using slang, allusion, metaphor, jokes, and unfamiliar references.
- Check often for comprehension. The presenter should maintain eye contact and question students directly about points which have been covered.

- Use visual aids such as posters and handouts to make the presentation more effective. Students in general will often learn more quickly with exposure to visual aids; this is especially true of foreign students, many of whom come from cultures where learning takes place through observation and emulation.[15]

Macdonald and Sarkodie-Mensah espoused the use of code switching, an important technique employed by ESL instructors and others involved in international education:

> The elements of the appropriate code (really a functional variety of English) are quite simple and obvious: repetition abounds; no particular words are automatically taboo, but common sense and experience help eliminate items that are not frequently found in the ESL student's vocabulary (*taboo*, for example, is a taboo word); technical words that should be mastered are defined in a carefully controlled vocabulary; all slang is avoided; there is a distinct preference for the Anglo-Saxon over the Latinate; rate of speech is slowed down and articulation enhanced but not to the point of exaggeration. This code is self-taught, based on a constant self-awareness of language when addressing foreign students and from trial and error with different groups.[16]

Care needs to be taken to maintain the presentation at the appropriate level and not to allow condescension to be perceived.

The individual differences in exposure to libraries, educational experiences, and learning styles described above must also be considered. In order to devise more successful teaching strategies, librarians and teachers must understand the backgrounds, abilities, and expectations of their international students. Since "the very conception of using books and research materials may be quite different" in other cultures, this understanding can become critical in library instruction.[17]

The most effective programs are those that employ a variety of approaches to library instruction and orientation.

These might include welcoming letters to new students, orientation programs and tours, formal course-integrated instruction, workbooks, and glossaries designed for international students.[18]

Staff Training

As critical as developing programs to teach international students how to use libraries can be, even more important is preparing library staff to communicate effectively with these students. Librarians must take the responsibility for bridging the communication gap which often serves as an insurmountable barrier between these students and the resources that they need.[19]

Staff development programs to increase cultural understanding, enhance communication skills, and expand teaching techniques form an essential component of library programs for international students on a number of campuses. At a minimal level, articles on the international-student experience in United States libraries, focus groups and lectures by international students to library staff, and attendance by library staff at international-program staff meetings are suggested for staff orientation to these issues.[20]

At the University of Arizona, an intensive workshop was developed to train library staff to communicate more effectively with international students. The specific goals of these workshops were:

- to have the participants experience some of the pressures inherent in trying to understand concepts and words in a second language;
- to encourage the participants to feel some of the emotions associated with culture shock;

- to lead the participants into an awareness of their own cultural assumptions and interpretations;
- to show the participants some typical culture differences (demonstrated by an encounter at the reference desk) and some effective ways to handle intercultural communication; and
- to demonstrate how to be effective when dealing with students from other cultures, especially during large instructional sessions.[21]

A videotape introducing interlibrary loan procedures in a language other than English was presented, followed by a test on its contents. A cross-cultural simulation game was also used to demonstrate cultural differences and the difficulties brought about by incorrect assumptions. Lectures and role playing on the dynamics of intercultural communication at the reference desk and in the classroom were also included.

At the University of Michigan, some elements of the Arizona program were utilized, augmented by the study of stereotyping and role-playing exercises which illuminated the participants' expectations of libraries.[22] The University of California, Davis, also reported that library staff education is an integral part of their program, which focuses on improving cultural awareness and enhancing the ability of staff to recognize and understand the special needs of international students.[23]

International Students and Multicultural Students

Once extensive programs for international students have been developed, the temptation may exist to simply expand them to include multicultural students. This would be a mistake for several reasons. Not only do the needs of international students vary considerably from those of multicultural students, their entire approach to American higher education is based upon a fundamentally different perspective.

International students enter American colleges and universities with the expectation that as visitors in institutions of a foreign country, they will probably encounter obstacles in communication and understanding. Their journey to the United States for higher education is often a privilege, one frequently underwritten by government support. Language barriers trigger inevitable problems with communication which are recognizable by the students themselves and the Americans with whom they speak. Cultural differences are comprehended by many they meet and allowances are often made for misunderstandings. While the difficulties faced by international students should not be minimized, they are usually identified and addressed by the colleges and universities which they attend.

The barriers facing multicultural students are more subtle. These students are, of course, in their own country and entitled to participate fully in all aspects of its society. Discrimination on the basis of race and ethnicity has been a fact of life for most of them which continues to exist, albeit in sometimes elusive forms, in colleges and universities. Cultural differences and communication problems are discounted or entirely unrecognized by faculty and staff. Dominant-culture values and perspectives which fail to acknowledge multicultural contributions continue to permeate the curriculum in most colleges and universities. Programs which address the needs of multicultural students are just beginning to emerge as legitimate entities in institutions of higher education.

While the characteristics and needs of international students and multicultural students clearly vary along several dimensions, some of the techniques described above may be useful in considering the development of services and programs for a diverse student population. The role of individual differences in experience, communication style, and learning behavior in learning to effectively use libraries cannot be discounted.

The potential for frustration among both of these groups of students is high as they approach library services which may be unresponsive to their needs. The placement of the responsibility for changing this pattern is clearly on the librarian, and the opportunity for making a contribution to the educational experiences of international and multicultural students is apparent. As Jacobson pointed out, "by turning each reference exchange into an instructional opportunity, the librarian is sharing knowledge of the system with the student. The student then stands on more equal ground and is empowered to move through the system with a sense of control and empowerment."[24] If the goal of the librarian is to improve the academic success of *each* student by providing effective access to information and information resources, then adjustment of library programs to meet these varying needs is essential.

Notes

1.   Frances F. Jacobson, "Bibliographic Instruction and International Students," *Illinois Libraries* 70 (1988): 628-633; and Laura S. Kline and Catherine M. Rod, "Library Orientation Programs for Foreign Students," *RQ* 24 (1984): 210-216.

2.   Lizabeth A. Wilson, "Changing Users: Bibliographic Instruction for Whom?" in *The Evolving Educational Mission of the Library*, ed. Betsy Baker and Mary Ellen Litzinger (Chicago: Association of College and Research Libraries, 1992), 20-53.

3. Frank W. Goudy and Eugene Moushey, "Library Instruction and Foreign Students: A Survey of Opinions and Practices Among Selected Libraries," *Reference Librarian* 10 (1984): 215-226.

4. Gina Macdonald and Elizabeth Sarkodie-Mensah, "ESL Students and American Libraries," *College and Research Libraries* 49 (1988): 425-431.

5. Wendy Moorhead, "Ignorance Was Our Excuse," *College and Research Libraries News* 47 (1986): 585-587.

6. Sally G. Wayman, "The International Student in the Academic Library," *Journal of Academic Librarianship* 9 (1984): 336-341.

7. Louise Greenfield, Susan Johnston, and Karen Williams, "Educating the World: Training Library Staff to Communicate Effectively with International Students," *Journal of Academic Librarianship* 12 (1986): 227-231; and Wayman, 337-338.

8. Wayman, 339.

9. Greenfield, Johnston, and Williams, 229.

10. Kline and Rod, 211; and Jacobson, 629.

11. Terry Ann Mood, "Foreign Students and the Academic Library," *RQ* 22 (1982): 178; and Wayman, 340.

12. Jacobson, 629; Wayman, 340.

13. Joan Ormondroyd, "The International Student and Course-Integrated Instruction: The Librarian's Perspective," *Research Strategies* 7 (1989): 148-158; and Dick Feldman, "The International Student and Course-Integrated Instruction: The ESL Instructor's Perspective," *Research Strategies* 7 (1989): 159-166.

14. Boyd Koehler and Kathryn Swanson, "ESL Students and Bibliographic Instruction: Learning Yet Another Language," *Research*

Strategies 6 (1988): 148-160; Greenfield, Johnston, and Williams, 231; and Moorhead, 585-587.

15. Greenfield, Johnston, and Williams, 230.

16. Macdonald and Sarkodie-Mensah, 428.

17. Ibid, 426.

18. Jacobson, 633; Wayman, 338.

19. Irene Hoffman and Oprista Popa, "Library Orientation and Instruction for International Students: The University of California-Davis Experience," *RQ* 25 (1986): 356; and Greenfield, Johnston, and Williams, 227.

20. Mood, 178.

21. Greenfield, Johnston, and Williams, 227.

22. Mary Alice Ball and Molly Mahony, "Foreign Students, Libraries, and Culture," *College and Research Libraries* 48 (1987): 160-166.

23. Hoffman and Popa, 356-358.

24. Jacobson, 632.

PART TWO

THREE INSTITUTIONS RESPOND

5
RESEARCH METHODOLOGY

Introduction

To study the emerging programs in academic libraries designed to meet multicultural student needs and to understand the factors which prompted their development, the programs on three university campuses were studied in depth. The analysis focused upon programs, services, attitudes, decisions, and resources within those libraries which relate to multicultural student needs. Although the behavior of individual librarians may also play a part in the development of these programs, this individual level of analysis was not considered in this study. In order to place these responses in a broader context, programs addressing multicultural student needs across each of the institutions were also explored.

A multiple-case study design was employed, using some of the features of embedded design described by Yin[1] to accommodate two levels of analysis in each case. The specific questions addressed in this research were:

- How are academic libraries responding to the changing demographics in the student population?
- How is the pattern of library responsiveness related to the institution's responses to diversity?

- What factors are associated with the development of academic library services that respond to the needs of multicultural students?
- Is a particular model of responsiveness more often associated with this response?

Case Study Sites

This research focuses on the responses of three academic libraries in different parts of the United States as each addresses the needs of multicultural students. One site, the University of California at Santa Cruz, was selected because of its reputation as having an innovative program to address multicultural student needs. In an effort to identify contrasting approaches, two similar institutions, the University of New Mexico and the University at Albany, State University of New York, were selected. These choices were made with geographic distribution and institutional access for the researcher in mind.

These predominantly Anglo institutions had multicultural student populations in 1991 of 20 to 33 percent. Each university is in a state whose population is quite diverse. In California and New Mexico, the percentage of high school graduates is projected to become more than 50 percent multicultural by 1995; New York's high school graduates are projected to be 30 percent multicultural by that time.[2] Demographic data for each state delineating race or ethnicity and two educational indicators are presented in Table 5.1.

The three case study institutions may be generally compared along several dimensions, as illustrated in Tables

5.2 and 5.3. The context of this study is undergraduate education at each of these universities, although programs responding to multicultural student needs at the graduate level were identified at some sites.

Table 5.1: Selected Demographic Data for Case Study States

CALIFORNIA

Ethnicity	1990 Population 18-24 Years	1988 High School Graduates	Fall 1988 Under-graduates
African American	9.2	7.7	5.5
Asian/Filipino	11.0	11.9	15.8
Hispanic	35.3	19.4	10.2
Native American	0.9	0.8	0.9
Anglo	54.1	60.2	64.1

NEW MEXICO

Ethnicity	1990 Population 18-24 Years	1988 High School Graduates	Fall 1988 Under-graduates
African American	2.4	1.9	2.1
Asian/Filipino	1.1	1.2	1.4
Hispanic	52.3	39.0	26.2
Native American	10.3	9.3	3.2
Anglo	47.7	48.6	65.6

**Table 5.1: Selected Demographic Data for Case Study
States** (Continued)

NEW YORK

Ethnicity	1990 Population 18-24 Years	1988 High School Graduates	Fall 1988 Under- graduates
African American	18.8	13.3	10.5
Asian/Filipino	4.6	3.4	4.8
Hispanic	16.8	7.4	6.4
Native American	0.4	0.2	0.3
Anglo	65.4	75.7	74.8

Source:　Western Interstate Commission for Higher Education and the College
Board, *The Road to College; Educational Progress by Race and Ethnicity*,
Boulder, CO: Western Interstate Commission for Higher Education, 1991.
Note: Data on the 1990 population by race/ethnicity, as quoted from this source, are
taken from the U.S. Bureau of the Census Public Law Data. The percentage of the 18-
to 24-year-old population by race/ethnicity is an estimate based on U.S. Bureau of the
Census unpublished ratios of the 18- to 24-year-old population by race/ethnicity for 1989
and the total 1990 population by race/ethnicity and state. As a result, discrepancies in
totals exist.

Interviews and Interviewees

The primary data presented in this study were gathered
in 1991/92 through approximately twenty on-campus
interviews at each of these universities. Those interviewed
in each library included: the library director or chief
administrative officer for the libraries, the head of public
service and/or reference service, the library instruction co-

Table 5.2: Selected University Characteristics, 1991

	Student Enrollment	Percent Multi-cultural	Under-graduates	1st-year Class
UCSC	10,100	30.5	9,130	1,840
UNM	24,000	33.2	19,500	1,780
SUNY-A	16,600	20.9	11,900	2,000

Table 5.3: Selected Library Characteristics, 1991

	Collection Size (in millions of volumes)	Staff Size	Annual Budget (in millions of dollars)
UCSC	1.0	130	6.9
UNM	1.4	144	8.4
SUNY-A	1.3	116	8.4

Source: Data presented in Tables 5.2 and 5.3 are derived from multiple sources
cited in each of the case studies.

ordinator, librarian(s) with responsibility for multicultural
services and ethnic studies collection development, and one
or two reference librarians. In order to develop a campuswide perspective, interviews were also conducted with
people holding the following positions at each campus:

senior administrators in academic affairs and student services, the affirmative action officer, admissions personnel with responsibility for multicultural recruitment, the learning assistance program director, student services personnel with responsibility for multicultural students, key faculty members in campus multicultural matters, the director of institutional research, and at least two multicultural students.

Two-page interview guides were developed for different categories of interviews based upon the research questions and components of the organizational responsiveness model. Areas covered included program description, campus issues and mission, response to campus demographics, perception of multicultural student needs, and perception of library role. Interviews followed these questions quite generally, in some cases leading to broad-ranging discussions of related topics. Probing questions were used to elicit specifics when responses were not forthcoming, and follow-up questions were used to verify information received from other respondents and to direct the discussion along specific lines of inquiry. Related written material and data were requested from each of those interviewed.

It should be noted that the following data describe programs and circumstances as they existed on these campuses during 1991 and 1992. These libraries are continuing to work on responses to multicultural students and have undoubtedly changed some features of their programs since this time.

Notes

1. Robert K. Yin, *Case Study Research; Design and Methods* (Newbury Park, CA: Sage Publications, 1989), 50-60.

2. Western Interstate Commission for Higher Education and The College Board, *The Road to College; Educational Progress by Race and Ethnicity* (Boulder, CO: Western Interstate Commission for Higher Education, 1991), 53-97.

6
CASE STUDY
UNIVERSITY OF CALIFORNIA, SANTA CRUZ

Background

The University of California at Santa Cruz is one of nine campuses in the University of California system. It was founded in 1965, with a vision to combine the University of California's strengths in scholarship and research with a focused emphasis on undergraduate education. Throughout its twenty-eight-year history, this campus has been known for distinctive approaches and experimentation in academic programs, student evaluation, and residential-college organization.[1] UCSC is located in a rural setting near the city of Santa Cruz, which has a population of 49,000. The surrounding community is largely Anglo, with some Hispanic populations in the nearby cities of Watson-ville, Salinas, and San Jose.

UCSC is one of the smaller campuses in the University of California system, with 10,100 students, of whom 960 are graduate students, and 419 faculty members in 1991.[2] Growth has been a major issue, with campus size increasing during the 1980s and scheduled to grow to 15,000 students by 2005.[3]

The state policy environment related to diversity in higher education in California has been especially strong, with the legislature playing a key role as early as 1968.[4] In 1989, the legislature's review of the California Master Plan for Higher Education singled out demographic and multicultural issues as the overriding priority for its colleges and universities.[5] In the nine-campus University of California system, this impetus is best captured in a letter from the University's president to the nine campus chancellors in 1988 which began:

> [I]t is essential that we reaffirm our commitment to encompass the cultural, ethnic, and racial richness of our state more fully within the University of California community. This commitment, which I know we all share, will command an even greater, indeed re-invigorated, effort on all of our parts owing to the rapidity of change that is occurring in the racial and ethnic mix of the state's populations.[6]

This letter, which charged the chancellors with specific responsibilities, was widely circulated on the UC Santa Cruz campus and became the focus of numerous campus responses.

The current campus demographics reflect considerable diversity when compared with similar campuses nationwide, although the student body is less diverse than other UC campuses. The multicultural undergraduate population has grown from 18.3 percent in 1982 to 30.5 percent in 1991. The composition of the Fall 1991 undergraduate class was 3.0 percent African American, 8.7 percent Asian, 1.5 percent Native American, 11.7 percent Hispanic, 3.3 percent Filipino, 2.1 percent other minority, and 69.8 percent Anglo.[7] The proportion of multicultural faculty members in 1991 was 18.8 percent overall, 31.6 percent of whom were at the assistant professor level.[8] The figures for multicultural staff were 25 percent at the executive level, 22.7 percent for academic and professional staff, and 30.1 percent for support staff.[9]

The campus response to this shift in demographics was explored through interviews with key individuals covering program descriptions and personal observations. These interviews took place during 1991.

Campus Response to Diversity

Mission

Multiculturalism is clearly a central concern on the Santa Cruz campus, and was positively identified by all parties interviewed as an important stated mission of the university. The 1991-92 *General Catalog* included many references to diverse ethnic and cultural backgrounds and experiences, and the mission statement for each of the eight colleges included a statement on these issues.[10]

In 1982, the UCSC Faculty Senate passed a set of resolutions based upon the premise that excellence in education would not be possible without diversity in the student body, in the faculty, and in the curriculum. The ethnic studies requirement, the Target of Opportunity faculty hiring program, and many of the increased recruitment efforts grew directly from these resolutions. Thus, the growing emphasis on multiculturalism came from the faculty instead of being initiated at the level of the chancellor or president and forced upon the campus community. Several administrators interviewed stated that this early faculty involvement, considered the source of the local multicultural movement, may be unique to this university site.

Table 6.1: Undergraduate Enrollment
(Fall 1972 and

Fall Quarter	African American	Asian	American Indian	Chicano	Latino
1991	3.0% 256	8.7% 749	1.5% 126	7.8% 665	3.9% 332
1990	3.0% 254	8.4% 718	1.3% 111	7.0% 602	3.3% 284
1989	3.1% 261	7.9% 671	1.2% 104	6.2% 527	2.9% 248
1988	2.8% 230	8.8% 731	0.9% 74	5.3% 440	2.7% 223
1987	2.5% 199	9.4% 749	0.8% 62	5.2% 418	2.4% 191
1986	2.6% 196	9.9% 750	0.6% 45	5.2% 389	1.9% 145
1985	2.2% 149	10.7% 710	0.6% 43	5.1% 338	1.6% 105
1984	2.7% 164	9.3% 573	0.5% 31	4.6% 285	1.5% 92
1983	2.7% 161	6.9% 417	0.6% 34	4.7% 280	1.6% 94
*	*	*	*	*	*
1972	2.8% 121	4.4% 188	0.6% 26	5.5% 236	1.0% 45

† not a separate ethnic category.
Note: East Indian Pakistani was moved from "Other Minority" to "Asian" as of fall 1984.

By Ethnicity
Fall 1983-1991)

Filipino	Other† Minority	Cau- casian	Subtotal: Ethnicity Available	Not Avail- able	Total
3.3% 282	2.1% 181	69.8% 5,984	100.0% 8,575	586	9,161
2.5% 214	2.0% 172	72.4% 6,188	100.0% 8,543	546	9,089
1.9% 160	1.8% 153	74.9% 6,334	100.0% 8,458	425	8,883
1.3% 111	1.9% 157	76.3% 6,316	100.0% 8,282	377	8,659
1.1% 91	1.9% 148	76.8% 6,139	100.0% 7,997	351	8,348
0.9% 70	2.0% 154	76.8% 5,790	100.0% 7,539	328	7,867
0.8% 54	1.6% 109	77.3% 5,141	100.0% 6,649	333	6,982
0.8% 51	2.1% 127	78.5% 4,830	100.0% 6,153	403	6,556
0.7% 42	2.4% 143	80.5% 4,839	100.0% 6,010	336	6,346
*	*	*	*	*	*
NA	1.1% 47	84.6% 3,653	100.0% 4,316	160	4,476

Source: University of California, Santa Cruz, Office of Planning and Budget, *Enrollment Fact Sheets, Fall 1991* (1991).

Formal campus planning documents also featured cultural diversity prominently in mission statements and planning goals. The *Twenty-Year Plan*, written in 1985, included as one of seven goals, "establish support programs that increase enrollment of underrepresented minorities."[11] *Draft Plan 2005*, a more recent document still under discussion on the campus, included this more encompassing statement, highlighting the importance of diversity issues:

> As an important part of the campus mission, UCSC should recognize and address the following first-order problems and opportunities that face the state and the nation: ethnic and cultural diversity, the environment, education, technology, and global education.[12]

Three major issues were repeatedly identified by those interviewed as heading the university's agenda: budget reductions, diversity, and growth. Growth had been widely discussed, with environmental concerns, increased anonymity, and community pressures dominating divisive campus debates on plans for the future.

Student Recruitment

Recruitment of multicultural students is a joint effort of the Student Affirmative Action/Equal Opportunity Program and the Admissions Office. From 1982 to 1991, enrollment of undergraduate multicultural students nearly doubled, while overall undergraduate enrollment grew by only 45 percent (see Table 6.1).[13]

The Assistant Dean of Admissions and others attributed this increase to outreach work beginning at the middle school level, as well as focused contact with potential students during the application period. Specific efforts included an ethnically diverse admissions staff, staff members with primary responsibility for multicultural outreach, intense support in the financial aid application process, and organized contact between faculty members and potential students. Admissions activities targeting economically disadvantaged students have received considerable funding during the past several years, and this priority has been being protected in the recent budget reductions.

Santa Cruz has been less successful than other University of California campuses in attracting multicultural students.[14] Although the numbers of multicultural high school graduates are growing rapidly in the state, the pool of qualified applicants is relatively low and the competition with the larger UC campuses and private institutions is stiff. In addition to competition and eligibility, barriers to initial enrollment include the inability of most multicultural students to attend UCSC while continuing to live at home, the pastoral setting, and the lack of a surrounding multicultural community.

Faculty Recruitment

The recruitment of faculty of color has been a priority for many years. A senior administrator with the joint appointment of Assistant Academic Vice Chancellor and Assistant to the Chancellor was given the responsibility for a range of issues in this area in the early eighties. She is responsible for academic personnel, faculty relations, and faculty hiring, as well as affirmative action. This is import-

Table 6.2: Statistics On Ladder Rank

	Professorial Position	Male	
		White	Minority
ARTS	Assistant (12)	4 (33.3%)	3 (25.0%)
	Associate (8)	4 (50%)	0
	Full (23)	16 (69.6%)	3 (13.0%)
	Total: (43)	**24 (55.8%)**	**6 (14.0%)**
HUMANITIES	Assistant (24)	6 (25.0%)	3 (12.5%)
	Associate (30)	11 (36.6%)	5 (16.7%)
	Full (46)	30 (65.2%)	4 (8.7%)
	Total: (100)	**47 (47.0%)**	**12 (12.0%)**
NATURAL SCIENCES	Assistant (41)	22 (53.7%)	7 (17.1%)
	Associate (18)	12 (66.7%)	2 (11.1%)
	Full (99)	85 (85.9%)	7 (7.1%)
	Total: (158)	**119 (75.3%)**	**16 (10.1%)**
SOCIAL SCIENCES	Assistant (40)	12 (30.0%)	8 (20.0%)
	Associate (24)	10 (41.7%)	3 (12.5%)
	Full (54)	38 (70.4%)	4 (7.4%)
	Total: (118)	**60 (50.8%)**	**15 (12.7%)**

Faculty As Of 7/1/91

Female		Total	
White	Minority	Female	Minority
5	0	5	3
(41.6%)		(41.6%)	(25.0%)
3	1	4	1
(37.5%)	(12.5%)	(50.0%)	(12.5%)
4	0	4	3
(17.4%)	___	(17.4%)	(13.0%)
12	**1**	**13**	**7**
(28.0%)	**(2.3%)**	**(30.2%)**	**(16.3%)**
9	6	15	9
(37.5%)	(25.0%)	(50.0%)	(30.0%)
13	1	14	6
(43.3%)	(3.3%)	(46.7%)	(20.0%)
8	4	12	8
(17.4%)	(8.7%)	(26.1%)	(17.4%)
30	**11**	**41**	**23**
(30.0%)	**(11.0%)**	**(41.0%)**	**(23.0%)**
10	2	12	9
(24.4%)	(4.9%)	(29.3%)	(22.0%)
4	0	4	2
(22.2%)		(22.2%)	(11.1%)
7	0	7	7
(7.1%)	___	(7.1%)	(7.1%)
21	**2**	**23**	**18**
(13.3%)	**(1.3%)**	**(14.6%)**	**(11.4%)**
12	8	20	16
(30.0%)	(20.0%)	(50.0%)	(40.0%)
5	6	11	9
(21.0%)	(25.0%)	(45.8%)	(37.5%)
10	2	12	6
(18.5%)	(3.7%)	(22.2%)	(11.1%)
27	**16**	**43**	**31**
(22.9%)	**(13.5%)**	**(36.4%)**	**(26.3%)**

Table 6.2: Statistics On Ladder Rank

	Professorial Position	Male White	Male Minority
CAMPUS TOTALS	Assistant (117)	44 (37.6%)	21 (18.0%)
	Associate (80)	37 (46.3%)	10 (12.5%)
	Full (222)	169 (76.0%)	18 (8.0%)
	Total: (419)	**250 (59.7%)**	**49 (11.7%)**

ant not only operationally but as a continuing signal to the campus of the importance of these issues.

Faculty affirmative action efforts have been made part of basic recruitment procedures, with deans expected to monitor searches for compliance. Deans review and sign off at each decision stage and the Assistant Vice Chancellor reviews searches before final appointment decisions. She also reviews all tenure and promotion decisions for equity of treatment and process before action is taken. Although intervention has rarely been necessary, the placement of this review in the Chancellor's Office provides greater influence and ensures that many issues are dealt with before they reach this level.

Many interviewed credited the Target of Opportunity program with much of the success in attracting multicultural faculty. Each year, several positions are identified for this program; they are not allocated to departments or specifically defined in terms of qualifications. Some years these positions have come from new allocations generated by enrollment growth; more often they have been reallocat-

Faculty As Of 7/1/91 (Continued)

	Female		Total	
White	Minority		Female	Minority
36	16		52	37
(30.8%)	(13.7%)		(44.4%)	(31.6%)
25	8		33	18
(31.3%)	(10.0%)		(41.3%)	(22.5%)
29	6		35	24
(13.1%)	(2.7%)		(15.8%)	(10.8%)
90	30		120	79
(21.5%)	(7.2%)		(28.6%)	(18.8%)

Source: University of California, Santa Cruz, Office of the Academic Vice
Chancellor, *Statistics on Ladder Rank Faculty as of 7/1/91* (1991).

ed from existing department vacancies. Departments
identify potential candidates who would meet general programmatic objectives and also fit ethnic diversity needs and
then propose a slate for consideration. A panel of faculty
select the best from these proposals with selection based
upon the qualifications of the individual rather than a
specific position description.

A total of thirty appointments have been made through
this program, with twenty-three continuing on the faculty
in 1991. The Assistant Academic Vice Chancellor believes
that the program has had an enormous halo effect, getting
faculty search committees in touch with networks and
improving all hiring pools. As a result, the hiring of
women and multicultural faculty through the traditional
departmental recruitment process has also increased.

The results of these efforts have been impressive. In
1991, no department had a faculty that was all Anglo male
and only two departments had faculties that were all Anglo.
The Academic Vice Chancellor stated that UCSC has the
most diverse faculty in the University of California system
and one of the most diverse in comparable research

universities nationwide. The Assistant Academic Vice Chancellor did not view retention of multicultural faculty as a major problem, despite the fact that she characterized the surrounding community as *terminally white* and pointed to a number of difficulties which faculty of color faced in making the decision to come to Santa Cruz. On the other hand, one librarian said that although the campus recruited faculty of color, they were not given sufficient support or power.

Staff Recruitment

Staff recruitment efforts, centered in the Affirmative Action Office, have also been enhanced in recent years. A new position for affirmative action recruitment and out-reach has been established in the Personnel Office, and vice chancellors have been asked to target positions for focused recruitment. The lack of a surrounding multicultural community continued to be a problem, because many people have not been willing to commute from more diverse population centers an hour away. However, there has been a gradual increase in multicultural hiring, and the Affirmative Action Officer suggested that the workforce was approaching the proportions of the local population.

Student Support Services

The Vice Chancellor for Student Services stated that until 1986, most of the emphasis relating to student diversity was placed on recruitment, with little attention to retention issues once the students arrived on campus. A major effort has been made to enhance academic support for multicultural students since that time. This support is being provided through Student Affirmative Action, which serves students belonging to underrepresented portions of California's diverse population, assisting Native-American, African-American, Filipino, and Hispanic students, and the Educational Opportunity Program, serving Californians from historically low-income backgrounds and those from communities with limited educational resources. The Vice Chancellor said that academic support programs for multicultural students were a high priority for student services, have received significant systemwide funding, and have been protected in budget cuts.

These services begin with a five-week summer bridge program for specially identified students needing intensive introduction to college life and academic expectations and an orientation program for all multicultural students providing opportunities for early academic advising, contacts with key faculty and staff, and information on the range of learning assistance programs available. Ongoing programs for continuing students include special advising and counseling services, an academic monitoring system, a peer advisor program, and a learning center with learning assistance and writing programs tied to academic disciplines. Faculty mentorship programs, research opportunities and a targeted outreach service are designed for students with potential for graduate studies. The majority of multicultural students participate in at least one of these programs.

One problem facing multicultural students has been the lack of ethnic communities in the area and the small multicultural community on the campus. Efforts to reduce alienation and strengthen the sense of campus community have included specially funded ethnic and cultural programming, special housing arrangements, and residential colleges focused on multicultural themes.

Curriculum and Pedagogy

Multicultural issues are reflected in the curriculum in several ways. An ethnic studies requirement for all students has been in place since 1986. In the 1991-92 catalog, this requirement was described in the following way:

> Ethnic/Third World Course. You must complete one course dealing with ethnic minorities in the United States or one course on a non-Western society. The intent of the requirement is to increase knowledge of non-Western cultures (in the U.S. and elsewhere), improve cross-cultural awareness, and explore relationships between ethnicity and other aspects of a liberal arts curriculum.[15]

Although no ethnic studies department exists, a wide array of options for special majors and studies in this area have been actively promoted through several interdisciplinary approaches.[16] College core courses, required of all first-year students, also have developed multicultural components and perspectives.

The Academic Vice Chancellor and others observed that the increase in multicultural faculty members has resulted in greater emphasis in research and teaching in diversity issues, because of the research focus that many of these individuals had brought with them. In the social sciences in particular, intellectual pursuit and program planning were closely related to demographic changes and societal transformation, with both diversity and globalization figuring prominently in programs and plans for future development.

Concern with respect to the importance of teaching in this regard was expressed by several faculty members interviewed. As the Dean of Social Sciences said, "The teaching is where the rubber hits the road." Issues of cultural style and sensitivity as well as curricular content in areas outside of ethnic studies were cited as important areas for improvement. Remedial support programs in the areas of language and writing have been imbedded in the curriculum, and the Academic Vice Chancellor hoped that, as a result, they would survive suggestions to transfer free-standing programs to the community colleges.

Campus Climate

Throughout the campus, there was concern expressed regarding the climate for multicultural students and faculty. While incidents of hate speech have not been as widely publicized as at some other universities, tensions do exist. The Academic Vice Chancellor said that the notions of cultural identity and cultural validation were troubling if carried to their ultimate extreme. How can we maintain multiple cultures and still forge a common culture through education? He considered that this was a complex issue where the factors of socioeconomic condition and class were involved.

Student affairs personnel stated that tension levels between multicultural students and Anglo students had not abated, but were becoming more subtle. Students interviewed felt that the climate was not as supportive as it should be, that a lot of lip service was being paid to multicultural issues.

The Affirmative Action Officer, also a faculty member, spoke of resistance to faculty of color as under the surface rather than openly hostile. Although there was widespread support for multiculturalism on the campus, the Dean of Social Sciences felt there were still many faculty questioning the substance and importance of diversity and its impact upon standards and quality.

Retention and Graduation

Retention rates across the campus have increased to a rate of 88 percent for return after one year, for students entering in 1989, and a rate of 76 percent for return after two years, for students entering in 1988. Retention rates for comparable periods were similar for African-American, Hispanic, and Asian students.[17] Forty-four percent of students entering in 1984 and 1985 graduated within five years, the highest five-year graduation rate in the last ten years. Graduation rates for Hispanic and African-American students were about seven percentage points lower than the campus average.[18]

Library Response

Background

The University Library has a collection of over one million volumes in two facilities: the McHenry Library and a new Science Library. As part of the statewide University of California library system, the University Library also serves as a gateway to millions of other books and periodicals on other campuses throughout the state.[19] In 1991, the staff consisted of thirty-two librarians and ninety-eight

Table 6.3: Retention and Graduation Rates; Five-Year Averages

	One Year	Two Year	Three Year	Four Year	Five Year	Six Year
African-American						
Retention	82.0	64.3	58.2	30.4	6.1	2.9
Graduation				14.4	29.7	34.1
Chicano						
Retention	85.6	69.0	58.8	35.5	4.8	3.1
Graduation				11.1	32.1	35.6
Hispanic/Latino						
Retention	83.6	76.5	71.1	45.4	10.6	4.5
Graduation				13.9	33.0	43.3
Asian						
Retention	89.4	70.1	62.8	32.5	8.7	3.1
Graduation				23.1	43.3	56.4
All Students						
Retention	85.8	69.4	62.6	28.3	6.5	3.0
Graduation				21.0	39.4	45.9

Note: The averages are based on the most recent five years of information. Thus, one-year retention rates include students who entered from 1985 to 1989; two-year rates are based on students entering from 1984 to 1988; three-year rates on students who entered from 1983 to 1987, and so on.

Source: The University of California, Santa Cruz, Office of Planning and Budget, *Retention and Graduation Update 1990-91* (1991).

support staff and the university budgeted $6.9 million for library operations.

The University Librarian dated the beginning of the library's active response to multicultural students to 1988, when multicultural student demands to the chancellor included a call for more library materials related to Asian-American heritage.[20] From the campus forum on these demands came the realization for the University Librarian and other librarians that they were not serving a substantial portion of the student body in the way that they were serving everyone else. Some librarians differed in their perceptions of when these needs were first recognized and asserted that efforts to promote multicultural issues in hiring, collection development, and reference service at the individual level preceded this event. However, the beginning of aggressive efforts to hire librarians of color and the creation of the position of Multicultural Services Librarian can be clearly pinpointed to this period.

Mission and Goals

Despite the Faculty Senate's 1982 resolution on diversity, the University Library's mission statement, written in the same year, included no recognition of this issue.[21] The first indication in formal written materials from the library was the goal established in 1988: "intensify efforts to hire [a] minority librarian."[22] After that time, annual goals statements included similar statements on hiring. In 1990, a goal related to cultural sensitivity training for staff was added, and in 1991, building and promoting ethnic studies collections appeared.[23] At the individual level, contributions to affirmative action and cultural diversity activities have been made part of every supervisory evaluation.

Policy Environment

The policy environment in the University of California system appeared to have an important impact upon the hiring efforts and program development at UC Santa Cruz. The University Librarian spoke of the growing influence of people of color who had moved into positions of power in fostering the realignment of the administration's perspective and in urging the university to do more in this area. He asserted that formal goals were not as important as the "sixteen different ways you get the message that you better be doing something, better be getting with the program." This perspective was reinforced by the perceptions of several librarians that the University Librarian was under considerable pressure to produce and that the influence of activities on other campuses, both within the UC System and elsewhere, was extensive.

Libraries within the University of California system have become increasingly active on multicultural issues, with UC Santa Cruz providing some of the leadership for these activities. In 1989, the Librarians Association of the University of California appointed an Ad Hoc Cultural Diversity Committee which held several statewide conferences and, in 1991, issued a report entitled *The Many Voices of Diversity*, with twenty-seven specific recommendations addressing collections, access, reference, instruction, and personnel.[24] The multicultural services librarian from UC Santa Cruz played a key role in the activities leading to this report.

Recruitment

Targeted recruitment of librarians of color has been an important part of the library's response to multicultural issues. From 1988 to 1991, two permanent positions were developed to attract multicultural candidates: a multicultural outreach librarian, a redefinition of a position within the reference department; and an ethnic studies bibliographer, a new position. In addition, two of the other four librarians hired for existing positions during this period were people of color. This brought the multicultural portion of the professional staff, which had been entirely Anglo prior to 1988, to 13 percent in 1991.[25]

Affirmative action recruitment was also a significant part of hiring at the support-staff level. Internal procedures were changed to require at least one multicultural candidate in every interview pool. However, the composition of the library supervisory and support staff, at 91 percent Anglo, is considerably less diverse than campuswide supervisory and support staff.[26]

Considerable efforts have also been made to hire students of color as part-time library employees. Student supervisors are specifically evaluated on their performance in this area. The increase in multicultural students in these visible positions, many of them on public service desks, was seen by library administrators and librarians as important in providing welcoming signs and role models for other students and in stimulating interest in potential careers in libraries.

Outreach Programs

The position of multicultural services librarian, based, as described above, on the realization that the multicultural students were not using the library, is dedicated specifically to outreach services. Many public libraries have extensive outreach programs developed by librarians who have the ability to communicate with, gain the trust of, and inspire those who are not reached by library services and then to tailor services to meet the needs of these people. However, academic libraries have traditionally functioned in a more passive role, serving those who come to the library and request assistance.

Recognizing the value of these outreach skills in the multicultural university environment, UC Santa Cruz hired a children's librarian from an urban public library to serve as their first multicultural services librarian in 1988. The initial position description included these duties:

> Responsible for providing leadership in library services for the campus multicultural community. Develops and coordinates an outreach program. Provides library instruction and specialized reference service in multicultural studies. Provides general reference service in the social sciences and humanities:...participates in computer reference service; prepares and presents instructional materials; selects reference materials....May be responsible for collection development in multicultural studies or another subject....[27]

At the time of this case study, this individual had left UC Santa Cruz, to pursue doctoral work, following three years in the position. The library was in the recruitment process to replace her (see Appendix A).

At the outset, the Multicultural Services Librarian visited the dorms once a month, inviting students of color to milk-and-cookies gatherings where they would feel comfortable enough to ask questions that they would not ask in the library. On a regular basis, she carried her outreach efforts into the campus community, visiting other agencies around the campus such as the residential colleges and the admissions, housing, and reentry offices. Her involvement in campuswide multicultural efforts helped to break down some of the barriers between the library and these students.

This librarian also developed and taught library instruction components for academic support programs for multicultural students, such as the Summer Bridge Program, Student Affirmative Action/EOP Orientation, and the Faculty Mentorship Program. She was the liaison to a residential college which focused on multicultural issues and worked cooperatively with the learning assistance programs. Her most intensive efforts were with the Faculty Mentorship Program, where she met with the program's thirty upper-division students each week to work on research skills and projects. She characterized her efforts as working outside the library to empower the students, thus creating demands on the library.

The impact of these programs was apparent to many of the individuals interviewed. Based upon anecdotal evidence confirmed by all those interviewed from the library, library use by multicultural students increased dramatically during this period. In addition, this new approach to service for these students once they reached the library raised questions of sensitivity and training for all those involved in public service.

Collections

In 1991, materials related to ethnic studies were dispersed throughout the library collections, rather than concentrated in centers as they are in some university libraries. This led to difficulties in identification of and access to resources, particularly in interdisciplinary topics. The University Librarian attributed the complaints about the lack of ethnic studies materials primarily to unawareness about the actual holdings of the library. Librarians observed that ethnic studies collections were quite uneven in depth and coverage. These holdings cannot compare to the resources of larger campus libraries such as UC Berkeley and UCLA, nor would it be reasonable to expect that they would do so.

The University Librarian suggested that the appointment of a new bibliographer to focus on ethnic studies would result in a more coordinated approach to building collections in this area. At the point of this case study, this individual had been working at UC Santa Cruz for only three months and was still in the process of evaluating existing resources. She identified the development of access tools for these collections as an initial goal. Resources for collection development were not specifically identified in the materials budget, but were part of a larger allocation for the social sciences.

Two small endowments for collections related to ethnic studies were established by 1991 in the areas of multicultural children's literature and Asian-American studies. These endowments were not large, $10,000 and $30,000 respectively, but the continuing income which they generate will help to protect these collections from inevitable budget cuts.

A reference librarian stated that the outreach programs and resulting library tours also caused library units with collection responsibilities to become more inclusive in their approaches to information and to increase their focus on diversity materials and issues. She observed that as areas such as Special Collections, Maps, and the Slide Library participated in orientation programs, they took steps to identify and promote their multicultural materials and to provide further diversification in building their collections.

Training

In early 1991, the library established a Task Force on Cultural Diversity. The University Librarian characterized this group as a grass-roots effort, with minimal liaison to administration. The mission which members of this task force had developed for themselves was:

> To develop a positive environment where all persons are able to achieve their full potential through acceptance and mutual respect among individuals, regardless of race, culture, status, gender, age, or lifestyle.[28]

According to the committee chair, a high priority for this group, which represented a cross section of the library, had been to develop a training program for the entire library staff in cultural diversity issues. The University Librarian identified funds to bring in an outside facilitator to conduct this program. In addition, the task force presented a series of panel presentations from campus community members from a variety of heritages and a video series on diversity issues.

Budgetary Support

In 1991/92, UC Santa Cruz spent approximately $683 per student for library support. Although no firm data at the campus level was available, the systemwide budget for the entire University of California system indicated that 3 percent of the operating budget for the nine university campuses was devoted to libraries.[29]

The library's budget for 1991/92 contained no line-item allocations for multicultural services or collections.[30]

However, two permanent professional positions, or 6 percent of the professional staff, were dedicated to multicultural services and collection development.

Issues

Perceptions of Need

While most librarians interviewed did not disagree with the goal to increase multicultural student use of the library, they differed in how they perceived the needs of these students. Many talked about the lack of comfort among multicultural students' approach to the library; these students were not using the library because they did not feel welcomed by the library or did not feel it was their library. This perception was confirmed by the students interviewed and by a counselor in academic support services.

Some librarians attributed this discomfort to differences of class rather than differences in race or ethnicity. One reference librarian said that students of color and Anglo working-class students had similar insecurities about requesting help at reference desks. She felt that affluent students of color were more like affluent Anglo students than they were like working-class students of color; exposure to library services and resources varied with these backgrounds, with discomfort occurring among those for whom the library represents an unknown. She found another important element to be the students' approach to the university in general: affluent students came in with an attitude that they had a right to be there, that they deserved the full range of resources and services; lower-class students, many of whom were the first in their families to attend college, were less confident about these issues. Another librarian agreed that class was a major issue, but commented that class combined with color created an even greater barrier to using libraries for many students.

In addition to a lack of experience with libraries, some librarians pointed to these students' lack of exposure to automation. One librarian said that Anglo students were certainly different in their comfort level with automation, which was important because there is no access to the library, not even a catalog, unless one could use a computer. He observed that this was a real disadvantage to multicultural students in general who seemed to be less computer-oriented than some of their Anglo classmates.

Other librarians questioned the assumption that multicultural students' needs and skill levels were different from those of majority students. One expressed discomfort with assuming that the library must come up with new ways to teach this special population something that they have never done before, because it presumed that the general population could do it. She felt that the differences in approach should be secondary to the basic needs for library skills for all students.

Impact on Service Approach

Librarians were questioned about the impact of increasing numbers of multicultural students on librarians' approaches to reference work and library instruction. For most, the major impact appeared to be in the latter area. Several librarians were rethinking their instruction methods, varying style and content based upon the composition of the class. The new techniques were often tied to uncovering perceptions about the library and the university, finding out "where the students are coming from," before the actual instruction session began. When working with groups including multicultural students, approaches tended to be more casual, to include more small-group activities, and to encompass more than one teaching style.

Reference service impacts were related to dealing with students' comfort levels and addressing the contents of their questions. The difficulties of finding information on diversity topics or multicultural perspectives on problems were raised repeatedly. Librarians talked about going to great lengths to find material and shifting paradigms to consider topics from non-traditional perspectives. One commented that a tenuous balance must be maintained between holding the student's interest and keeping him or her from becoming discouraged during this lengthy process. She suggested that it was important not to discount the question as too difficult to locate information on, leading the student to view it as an invalid or inappropriate topic. The overlay of issues of initial comfort with libraries and computerized information resources often complicated these interactions.

Isolation/Integration of Programming

Another issue which came up repeatedly was the decision to place all outreach activities and services developed to meet newly identified needs in the hands of one person. It appeared that widespread interest and excitement existed among the professional staff in working with multicultural students at the point that the first multicultural services librarian was hired. At the outset, some were involved in instructional activities such as the summer bridge program. However, as the activities of the Multicultural Services Librarian became more extensive, some of these librarians felt excluded. Formal participation by the reference librarians in these activities declined, and as students of color sought out the Multicultural Services Librarian when coming to the library a rift developed. One librarian went so far as to say that for many multicultural students, the Multicultural Services Librarian *was* the library. He said that she became the gateway to the library for multicultural students, and at times it was perceived that this role extended to becoming the gatekeeper. From her perspective, introduction to the library's services for these students was the key, and it was not unusual for them to follow up with the person with whom they began. She observed that the issue of service quality was also an element in this pattern of interaction.

This concern about the focus of services in one individual was shared by some outside the library who collaborated with the multicultural services librarian on programs for multicultural students. A counselor in the Student Affirmative Action/Equal Opportunity Program Office expressed the view that the entire organization needed to respond, that no one individual could be there twenty-four hours a day. Furthermore, she felt that support for multicultural students should be part of everyone's responsibility; it should be mainstreamed into the operations of the organization. At the same time, the importance of librarians of color as role models and as receptive professionals for students was emphasized by observers outside the library.

The issue of integration of multicultural services into public service programs for the entire library, but particularly in the reference department, received considerable attention in discussions leading up to the recruitment of a replacement for the multicultural services librarian. Some felt that although her role encouraged awareness in the library, because so much of her time was spent outside the library, she was isolated from regular interaction and input from other librarians.

With the hiring of the new librarian for this position, the reference department hoped to establish a team approach to the programs that had been developed. During the interim, the mentorship program was restructured to include assignment of students to librarians with subject specialties related to their research interests. All interested librarians were being encouraged to become involved in instructional activities. The need for the outreach activity assigned to one individual still existed, but the response to the needs, once identified, would become more collaborative, according to those interviewed.

Resources and Trade-Offs

In an environment of declining resources, the issue of support for new services was sure to arise, and this library was no exception. Although the University Librarian contended that no resources were diverted to support the positions and programs targeting multicultural students, some librarians perceived that as the priorities shifted, the focus on services for the broader population had weakened. The program of systematic library instruction for all undergraduates was restructured to address more specific groups and needs. However, hours of reference service were reduced, partly in response to other demands being placed on professional staff time.

The University Librarian and several others raised questions regarding service priorities. Should the emphasis be placed upon drawing non-users into the library or on serving those individuals who are already there, requesting service? Are the skills and knowledge bases of the entire student population sufficient to assume that most can handle the library on their own, allowing a focus on those needing extra assistance?

In addition, the role of the multicultural services librarian as a professional person of color on the campus-at-large raised questions of time allocation and priorities. In working closely with some multicultural students, she became a confidante and informal counselor on both academic and personal issues. She was also actively involved in cultural sensitivity training for a wide variety of campus organizations. While this heightened visibility for the library across the campus, the time involved was perceived to increase the demand on those left to run basic library services.

Continuing Demand for Collections

The demand for materials related to ethnic studies, identified by the University Librarian in 1988 as an impetus for change, had not dissipated in 1991. Several articles appeared in the campus newspaper *City on a Hill* in 1988, 1989, and 1991, reflecting this continuing demand.[31] Two individuals interviewed indicated that a caucus of Chicano faculty and students was about to release a report containing very critical remarks regarding library holdings in this area.

The library's primary response to these demands was to improve access to existing collections through outreach and instructional services, rather than to substantively strengthen the collections of the library. While the access issue was prominent in library discussions of the situation, the problem of collection deficiencies continued to arise.

One librarian observed that this demand for materials was due not only to increased interest by multicultural students in topics related to their heritages, but to shifts in the curriculum itself. She said that at the reference desk, student demands had begun to take the form of expectations, due to more and more syllabi focused on world cultures and on gender, class, and race intersections, especially for first-year core courses. She observed that the multicultural curriculum meant that the library necessarily had to respond; the demand was a result of student assignments, not just of student interest.

Perceptions of Library Responsiveness

As indicated above, students appeared to believe that the library had no material related to their topics of interest, while librarians asserted that the materials were there, just difficult to find. Several librarians observed that comfort levels in using the library became barriers for students, even though personal assistance and service were available to them if they asked. The Ethnic Studies Bibliographer asserted that whether or not collections and services were available was not the issue; if students perceived that they were not there, they might as well have been absent.

Outreach services may have begun to change these perceptions. Many interviewed from outside the library commented on the active involvement and high visibility of the outreach programs. The Assistant Vice Chancellor said, "Suddenly, the library was everywhere." The Academic Vice Chancellor talked about the symbolic importance of an accessible library in the overall campus response to multicultural students. One student discussed the change in her perspective of the library as a cold, unsupportive place to an important resource for her research.

Conflict

The development of services to meet multicultural student needs did not come without cost to the UC Santa Cruz library. The Multicultural Services Librarian raised many issues which caused discomfort among library staff. The trade-off issue on whom to serve was just one of these. Cultural insensitivity, communication styles, assumptions about individuals, and value-laden approaches to information were just a few of the potential barriers to library service which were actively debated by this staff. Volatile and divisive issues such as racism, favoritism, and fairness characterized some of these interactions. This difficult process, at considerable personal cost to several persons including the Multicultural Services Librarian, seemed to have resulted in more systemic awareness and change in approach for the library.

Notes

1. University of California, Santa Cruz, Office of Admissions, *UC Santa Cruz* (1990).

2. University of California, Santa Cruz, *General Catalog, 1991-92* (1991), 6.

3. University of California, Santa Cruz, Committee on 2005, *Draft Plan 2005* (22 January 1992), 6.

4. Richard C. Richardson and Elizabeth Fisk Skinner, *Achieving Quality and Diversity; Universities in a Multicultural Society* (New York: Macmillan, 1991), 151.

5. California, Legislature, Joint Committee for Review of the Master Plan for Higher Education, *California Faces...California's Future; Education for Citizenship in a Multicultural Democracy* (Sacramento, CA: Joint Legislative Publications Office, 1989).

6. David Pierpoint Gardner, President of the University of California, to Chancellors, 26 September 1988.

7. University of California, Santa Cruz, Office of Planning and Budget, *Enrollment Fact Sheets, Fall 1991* (1991), 5.

8. University of California, Santa Cruz, Office of the Academic Vice Chancellor, *Statistics on Ladder Rank Faculty as of 7/1/91* (1991).

9. University of California, Office of the President, Office of Business and Employment Affirmative Action, *Executive Program Representation, MAP Program Representation, A&PS Program Representation, Staff Personnel Program Representation, by Location, Ethnicity and Sex* (April 1991).

10. University of California, Santa Cruz, *General Catalog*, 6, 19, 31-32, 59-69.

11. University of California, Santa Cruz, *Twenty-Year Plan; Summary* (July 1985), 1.

12. University of California, Santa Cruz, Committee on 2005, *Draft Plan 2005*.

13. University of California, Santa Cruz, Office of Planning and Budget, *Enrollment Fact Sheets*, 10.

14. University of California, Santa Cruz, Office of Planning and Budget, *Retention and Graduation Update 1990-91* (1991), 23.

15. University of California, Santa Cruz, *General Catalog*, 26.

16. University of California, Santa Cruz, Divisions of Humanities and Social Sciences, *U.S. Ethnic Studies, 1990-91* (1990).

17. University of California, Santa Cruz, Office of Planning and Budget, *Retention and Graduation Update*, 4-8.

18. Ibid., 1.

19. University of California, Santa Cruz, *General Catalog*, 47.

20. Allan J. Dyson, "Reaching Out for Outreach; a University Library Develops a New Position to Serve the School's Multicultural Students," *American Libraries* 20 (1989): 952-54.

21. University of California, Santa Cruz, University Library, *University Library Mission and Objectives* (26 May 1982).

22. University of California, Santa Cruz, University Library, *1988 Goals Meeting Report* (13 September 1988).

23. University of California, Santa Cruz, University Library, *1989 Goals Meeting Report* (22 August 1989), *1990 Goals Meeting Report* (13 March 1990), and *1991 Goals Meeting Report*, (26 February 1991).

24. Librarians Association of the University of California, *The Many Voices of Diversity; Report of the Ad Hoc Committee on LAUC Regional Workshops on Cultural Diversity in Libraries* (1991).

25. Communication from Cheryl Gomez, 9 December 1991.

26. Ibid.; and University of California, Santa Cruz, Office of the President, Office of Business and Employment Affirmative Action, *Staff Personnel Program Representation*, 1.

27. University of California, Santa Cruz, University Library, "Multicultural Services Librarian" (10 June 1988).

28. University of California, Santa Cruz, University Library, *Cultural Diversity Task Force Minutes* (5 August 1991).

29. University of California, Office of the President, *1991-92 Budget for Current Operations* (October 1990).

30. University of California, Santa Cruz, University Library, *Final Recommended 1991/92 Library Budget* (8 August 1991).

31. *City on a Hill*, 28 January 1988, 26 May 1988, 26 January 1989, 10 October 1991.

7
CASE STUDY
UNIVERSITY OF NEW MEXICO

Background

The University of New Mexico, founded in 1889, is the flagship campus in New Mexico's public university system. A comprehensive research university, it serves over 24,000 students on its main campus in Albuquerque, 4,500 of them at the graduate level. The university supports programs in 170 accredited disciplines, with baccalaureate degrees in more than 120 fields, master's degrees in 59 fields, and doctoral degrees in 35 fields. UNM ranks among the top fifty American universities in terms of federal support for research, with over 84 million dollars in external support awarded annually to faculty and staff for research, public service projects, and sponsored instruction. The university is located in the center of Albuquerque, a metropolitan area with a population of 460,000.[1]

The state of New Mexico, which prides itself on its multicultural heritage and population, has long had diverse representation in the legislature and the statehouse. Access and success of people of color in higher education have been very prominent policy issues for the New Mexico legislature since the early 1980s.[2] In 1988, in response to a legislative directive, the New Mexico Commission on

Higher Education published a statewide policy imperative on these issues entitled *Planning for the Class of 2005: A Vision of the Future*. This report, citing demographic projections and state economic development, calls for participation of students, faculty, and administrators in higher education to reflect New Mexico's demography equitably.[3]

In 1991, House Memorial 38 (a memorial in New Mexico is a resolution in other states) resulted in an action plan, *Increasing Participation and Success of Minority Students in Postsecondary Education*, with specific statewide goals and strategy checklists for each institution. The goal of equity in this plan is clear:

> This is a plan—and a statewide commitment—to equalize educational opportunity and achievement for all ethnic groups composing New Mexico's citizenry....In most education communities, there remains clear underrepresentation of Hispanic and Native American students and in some instances Black or Asian students. This plan is proposed as another step toward helping all communities of the state to achieve parity of educational opportunity for all students: educational achievement determined by the abilities and interests of each student, not by the ethnic group he or she represents.[4]

The University of New Mexico, which figures prominently in both of these reports, is cited in the latter as having "the most fully defined plan for cultural diversity in the state—The New Mexico Plan."[5]

The ethnic composition of this large student body remained virtually constant for the past fifteen years, with the multicultural population recorded at 33.5 percent in 1977 and 35.2 percent in 1991. The entire enrollment for Fall 1991 was comprised of 4.2 percent Native-American, 2.2 percent African-American, 2.1 percent Asian, 25.7

percent Hispanic, 64.8 percent Anglo, and 1.0 percent foreign students.[6] The first-year class in 1991 was 39.9 percent Hispanic, which exceeded the proportions in the state's graduating high school class for the same year. Both Native-American and Hispanic enrollments are among the highest in the country for comprehensive research universities. With an average age of 25, more than 60 percent of the undergraduates are from Albuquerque or the surrounding Bernalillo County, and most work part-time and continue to live at home.[7]

Diversity among the faculty and staff has been less pronounced, particularly at the higher levels. Although the proportion of Hispanic faculty, at 8 percent in 1991, dramatically exceeded the national availability rate of 2 percent,[8] the overall segment of the faculty comprised of people of color was only 13.7 percent. The 1991 workforce composition at the support-staff level was 61 percent multicultural, greater than local availability. However, the higher ranks showed more disparities with the surrounding population, with 28 percent multicultural representation among the professional staff and 26 percent representation at the executive level.[9]

The campus response to this diverse population was explored through interviews with key individuals covering program descriptions and personal observations. These interviews took place during the spring of 1992.

Campus Response to Diversity

Mission

The mission of the University of New Mexico, as reflected in many public documents, clearly includes multiculturalism as a top priority. *UNM 2000*, a comprehensive campus plan completed in November 1990, identified diversity as a core institutional value and contained opening statements on the commitment to establish the university's "leadership in securing the fullest participation of Hispanics, African Americans, Native Americans, Asian Americans and European American women in the full range of academic functions and roles," and to become "a model of diversity."[10] Admissions materials promoted UNM's "multicultural population,"[11] and the 1991-93 catalog listed among nine university goals recruiting, admitting, and retaining students from elements of the state's populations underrepresented in its programs, taking advantage of the unique opportunities offered by the state's rich history and multicultural society to shape its programs, and acting affirmatively in the selection of faculty and staff in order to improve ethnic representation.[12]

The university's *New Mexico Plan*, 1991, characterized UNM as "a leader in the national effort to bring previously excluded groups into the university," and a multicultural campus where "diversity is explored and celebrated as one of [its] greatest assets." This plan included concrete programs for special intervention and special funding in the areas of early identification of potential university students, undergraduate student recruitment and retention, graduate students' issues, campus climate, and faculty development.[13]

In 1992, other major issues identified by those interviewed included campus planning, definition of priorities, and reallocation of resources. Although multiculturalism was seen as a key component by the university, most interviewees identified it as a campus priority only after probing questions.

Student Recruitment

The university's major efforts in the area of multicultural recruitment have taken place since 1987, coinciding with the end of a relatively open admissions plan. Prior to that time, primary outreach activities occurred as part of the College Enrichment Program, a federally funded program aimed at low-income, underprepared, and first-generation college students. *The New Mexico Plan* has earmarked funding and provided institutional commitment to a variety of early identification and intervention programs designed to attract students, primarily from in-state, to the university. Summer bridge programs, mother-daughter projects in several communities, and transfer student initiatives for branch campuses and community colleges have been among these efforts.[14]

In 1989, a group of multicultural students initiated the Minority Recruitment and Retention Program, through which UNM students actively recruit in the local high schools. According to the Assistant Vice President, Student Affairs, this program has been very successful, and since 1992, has been staffed with a full-time director funded by Student Affairs. Decentralized recruitment programs also have been in existence in academic units across the campus, most notably in the engineering and education colleges.

Recruitment efforts have been most successful with Hispanics, where UNM has been attracting more than its share of qualified graduating high school seniors in the state. The Director of Admissions and Student Outreach attributed this to proactive measures in local high schools, such as frequent interaction with the university community and on-site admissions at the high school. The presence of a significant Hispanic population among the student body

**Table 7.1: Regular Undergraduate Race-Ethnicity Percentages
1977-1990**

Year	Anglo	Hispanic	Native American	African American	Asian	Missing
1977	66.5	27.0	3.5	1.9	1.1	9.7
1978	67.1	26.4	3.5	1.9	1.1	7.1
1979	66.7	26.3	3.5	2.2	1.3	4.3
1980	68.0	25.1	3.3	2.2	1.4	2.7
1981	67.9	25.1	3.3	2.2	1.6	2.0
1982	67.2	25.8	3.2	2.1	1.7	1.7
1983	67.1	25.4	3.5	2.1	2.0	1.3
1984	65.9	25.9	3.9	2.2	2.0	1.1
1985	65.8	25.9	3.9	2.2	2.2	0.9
1986	66.4	25.4	3.6	2.1	2.4	0.8
1987	66.7	25.1	3.7	2.0	2.5	0.3
1988	67.9	24.1	3.7	1.8	2.5	0.2
1989	67.8	23.8	3.8	1.8	2.6	0.1
1990	66.6	24.7	3.9	2.2	2.5	0.2

Source: University of New Mexico, Planning and Policy Studies, *Selected Indicators on Students* (June 1991).

has also been a contributing factor. However, she also stated that UNM has not been getting its "state share" of qualified Native-American students. Although confirming data was not available, she and others interviewed speculated that many of these New Mexico residents attend tribal colleges, local institutions, or colleges having special financial arrangements with individual tribes.

Faculty and Staff Recruitment

Affirmative action has been a major campus issue due to a long Department of Labor investigation which was begun in response to two discrimination complaints filed in 1988, one by a group of Hispanic administrators followed by a class complaint from female faculty and administrators. Although the investigation did not ultimately prove discrimination in either case, the 1991 conciliation agreement required the establishment of compliant affirmative action plans and significant changes in faculty and staff employment procedures and record keeping.

The publicity surrounding these complaints heightened awareness on several levels. The Associate University Counsel said that once the complaints became public, "the legislature became vigilant, the press became critical, and the minority communities were up in arms." Political forces coalesced around this issue to force change. On the campus, affirmative action hiring became a primary concern, generating a comprehensive effort to integrate women and people of color in the populations of staff, faculty, and students. According to several of those interviewed, although pockets of serious resistance among the Anglo male faculty exist, there is widespread commitment to diversifying the institution.

The hiring process for faculty and professional staff has been augmented with search coordinators, usually senior faculty members, responsible for overseeing all aspects of the search. A formal initiative, the UNM Faculty Opportunity Hiring Program, was established to hire faculty who are highly qualified with special competencies for whom there are no existing vacancies. This program has as its emphasis the institutional priority of cultural diversity. It has been designed not as a new approach, but as an expansion of an existing strategy that formerly benefited only white males. Incentive funds have been provided centrally for positions and salary enhancements, although competitive packages have been difficult to offer in the tight fiscal environment. Of the new faculty hired in 1990-91, 23 percent were from underrepresented groups and 45 percent were female.[15]

At the staff level, hiring goals have been established by job category but not by department. The Director of Affirmative Action stated that this has caused some dissatisfaction among supervisors and has made it difficult for her office to focus on problem areas. The new compliance procedures, which are very detailed, have also created some resistance. Training for supervisors and others involved in the recruitment process has been identified as a high priority.

Table 7.2: Demographic Profiles of UNM Faculty

Number of Faculty

	1982	1986	1990	Change 1982-1990
Full-time	1,028	1,081	1,187	+15.5%
Part-time	258	367	370	+43.4%
Total	1,286	1,449	1,557	+21.1%
Total Number of Faculty Full-time Equivalents	1,101	1,195	1,366	+24.1%

Note: Faculty in these tables include those at the Main Campus, Medical School and Librarians with faculty status. Department Chairs are included. Excluded are teaching assistants, branch college faculty, and administrative personnel with faculty rank who are not chairs.

Table 7.2: Demographic Profiles of UNM Faculty (Continued)

Race/Ethnicity of UNM Faculty

	1982	1986	1990
% Anglo	90.5	89.6	86.4
% Hispanic	6.3	6.2	7.7
% Indian	0.6	0.7	0.6
% Black	0.6	0.4	0.8
% Asian	2.0	3.1	4.4

Source: University of New Mexico, Planning and Policy Studies, *UNM Faculty: Summary Data* (January 1991).

Student Support Services

The Division of Student Affairs has developed several programs which support multicultural students. Three ethnic-student service centers, American-Indian Student Services, Hispanic Student Services, and African-American Student Services, have been designed to provide whatever students need to be successful: peer and personal counseling, unofficial advising, tutoring, assisting with financial aid and other parts of the bureaucracy, and career planning and placement. With a focus on retention, these small centers, each with a staff of two, also have provided cultural support and social centers for multicultural students. Students have used these services on a voluntary basis, and their effectiveness was said to be uneven. Student Affairs also has been administering the Minority Recruitment and Retention Program, a student-run program of peer mentors working to improve retention.

The College Enrichment Program has served approximately 700 students annually who had low incomes, were underprepared, or were first-generation college students. Over 80 percent of these students have been from underrepresented groups. Support services have included offering special orientation programs, monitoring of academic progress, individual counseling and tutoring, and assisting with job placement.

The primary academic tutoring program has been located not in Student Affairs, but in the Library. The Center for Academic Program Support has provided free tutoring in all undergraduate subject areas as well as workshops in improving study and writing skills. This program will be covered in detail in the section on the library's response.

Curriculum and Pedagogy

Discussions with faculty and academic administrators indicated that evidence of a multicultural perspective in the curriculum has been mixed. No course has been required in this area, although such a component did exist in a preliminary core curriculum proposal which, at the time of this study, had not yet been approved by the faculty. The Associate Vice President, Academic Affairs, anticipated that this proposal was likely to be hotly debated from a number of sides. In addition to the expected opposition from conservative Anglo faculty espousing the traditional western canon, some Chicano Studies faculty were opposing the requirement on the basis that Chicano Studies is not a minority program at UNM and should not be treated separately from the mainstream curriculum.

A review of the college catalog revealed courses on multicultural issues across the curriculum. The Director of African-American Studies observed that some increase in such courses has been discernable over the past few years, but that the multicultural perspective usually has been focused in one course in a department and has not permeated the mainstream curriculum. However, the Associate Vice President, Academic Affairs, pointed to the appointment of new multicultural faculty as a growing source of multicultural approaches in traditional departments.

In 1992, ethnic studies programs existed in Chicano Studies, Native-American Studies, and African-American Studies. Only African-American Studies offered a formal degree program, with two structured minors and thirty-two courses at the undergraduate level. Native-American Studies was developing a bachelors degree option. The focus of Chicano Studies was to identify and develop a cadre of courses in other departments.

Campus Climate

In comparison to other campus environments experienced by some of those interviewed, the overall feeling was that the UNM climate appeared to be rather open. Interviewees did say that there have been some problems with fraternities and sororities which has resulted in a cultural awareness task force in the student association to address the issues campuswide. The focus of this group, as well as most of the multicultural student organizations, has been on awareness rather than protest.

The large Hispanic populations among the student body and the surrounding community were identified by some of those interviewed as important and unique factors contributing to the comfort level of these students on the UNM campus. Others characterized the university as continuing in the traditional model with high assimilation levels for some Hispanic students rather than an actual shift of the institution to a multicultural perspective.

Retention and Graduation

Retention rates of freshmen returning for the third semester have increased over the seven-year period from 63 percent in 1983 to 70 percent in 1990. There has been improvement in this rate for multicultural students, with percentages near the overall rate in all categories except Native Americans, where retention to the third semester is eight points below that for the total population. This disparity becomes even more pronounced in retention to the fifth semester, where the 1989-90 overall rate was 61 percent and the rate for Native-American students was 49 percent.[16]

In 1991, the median time to graduation from UNM was six years, with 28 percent of the 1985 entering freshman class graduating after twelve semesters. Approximately 6 percent of the student body completed an undergraduate degree program in four years, and 20 percent graduated after five years.[17] The large proportion of part-time students is a factor in these graduation rates.

Although the multicultural proportions of the student body remained relatively stable from 1977 through 1990, the percentages of students of color receiving degrees from the university increased. In 1977-78, 23 percent of the bachelors degrees awarded by UNM were to multicultural students; in 1989-90, this percentage rose to 31 percent.[18]

Table 7.3: Degrees Awarded by Race/Ethnicity For All Degrees 1977-78 through 1989-90 in Percentages

	African American	Asian	Native American	Hispanic	Anglo	Non-Res. Alien	No Response	Total
1977-78	1.1	1.2	3.3	17.1	77.3	0	0	2,978
1978-79	1.1	1.1	3.2	18.3	76.3	0	0	2,958
1979-80	1.4	2.0	2.4	19.2	75.0	0	0	2,999
1980-81	1.0	2.4	3.8	19.3	73.5	0	0	2,948
1981-82	1.2	2.2	4.9	18.2	73.6	0	0	2,902
1982-83	1.6	2.5	4.4	19.9	71.6	0	0	2,908
1983-84	1.4	2.3	3.5	19.5	73.3	0	0	2,832
1984-85	1.3	2.4	4.2	19.8	72.3	0	0	2,911
1985-86	0.9	3.0	3.4	21.8	70.9	0	0	3,073
1986-87	1.2	3.0	3.5	19.3	73.0	0	0	2,954
1987-88	1.5	2.8	3.0	19.7	73.0	0	0	3,060
1988-89	1.1	1.9	3.1	20.1	69.2	4.0	0.6	3,264
1989-90	1.2	2.1	3.2	19.3	69.6	4.2	0.4	3,363

Source: University of New Mexico, Planning and Policy Studies, *Comparison of Characteristics of Four Beginning Freshman Cohorts, Fall 1983 through Fall 1991* (October 1991).

Library Response

Background

The General Library at the University of New Mexico has a collection of more than 1.4 million volumes housed in five facilities, the Zimmerman Library and four subject-oriented branch libraries. Two specialized centers, the Center for Southwest Research and the Center for Academic Program Support (CAPS), are located in the Zimmerman Library. A staff of 43.5 library faculty and 100 support staff develop and process collections and provide a wide array of information services to the campus community.[19] In 1991, the UNM General Library was given a budget of $8.4 million for its operations.[20]

Mission and Goals

The most recent statements of mission and future directions for the library were contained in documents written by the Dean of Libraries to the Provost regarding budget reallocations and a forthcoming program review process.[21] The mission was framed by the statement regarding libraries in *UNM 2000*, which focused on the quality of the libraries as a measure of quality for the institution.[22] The importance of undergraduate education characterized by ethnic diversity was also cited for special attention. Key issues identified for exploration in the program review included "increasing multicultural diversity within the library faculty and the ability of the library to respond to multicultural diversity issues and educational needs."[23]

Another current objective related to diversity in these statements was that the library continue to be an "excellent freedom of information sanctuary for scholars, students, and others researching and learning about New Mexico and the greater Southwest."[24] The multicultural context of this state and the particular approach to its history in this library will be described later in this chapter.

However, discussion of library mission, goals, and priorities with the Dean of Libraries and with librarians yielded different results. Few identified multiculturalism as an important current issue for the library, even after several probing questions. The Dean of Libraries identified it as an item requiring study in the near future but could not assign it a priority at this time. Others said that awareness of the issue was increasing but that it was not yet a priority for the library.

A clearer area of development in the mission of the library is that of educational support. The Dean of Libraries stated that the library should not only support and complement the curriculum but should be actively involved in classroom instruction and tutoring. He would like to see the library become more of an educational center, the place where students go for all of their out-of-classroom learning. This philosophy is embodied in the mission of the Center for Academic Program Support, which strives to provide all out-of-classroom academic support for undergraduate students.

Policy Environment

The importance of multiculturalism in higher education in the statewide political environment has been a salient factor for the Dean of Libraries in recent planning. The transformation of the former special collections department into the Center for Southwest Research was prompted at least partly by the motivation to seek external funding. By focusing on the development of collections related to the many cultures of New Mexico and the Southwest, the library was able to establish itself as an important scholarly resource on the multicultural heritage of New Mexico and garner significant capital funding for an expansion of the Zimmerman Library.

Center for Southwest Research

The Center for Southwest Research is a library-based research and instructional facility designed to serve the needs of university and community members working in the area of the multicultural history of the Southwest. By expanding the focus of the special collections department (then largely an archive of rare books and manuscripts on the history of Anglos in New Mexico and on Latin American and Iberian studies), the Center has been active in providing opportunities for research that "actively discourage a selective or exclusionary presentation of the past."[25] (See Appendix B.)

These efforts include developing collections on indigenous peoples, supporting a major oral history program and other research projects, and engaging in active outreach to the community. Instructional sessions for undergraduate and graduate courses provide access to these resources for students engaged in exploring multicultural issues.

This center, a showcase on multiculturalism for the UNM Libraries, was identified as an important contribution to the university's efforts in multiculturalism by many interviewed both in the library and across the campus. The philosophy guiding this center was perhaps best described in the following quote from an article on its development:

> Academic libraries have an opportunity to contribute in significant ways to the questions raised in discussions of cultural pluralism. In cooperation with existing campus and community programs, university libraries have a responsibility to be in the forefront supporting curriculum and research activities that heighten the appreciation for the diversity in American life....By emphasizing a multicultural approach in developing the Center's collections and affiliated programs, we seek an active, participatory role in the reinterpretation of history.[26]

State and federal funds have been supporting a $7 million renovation and expansion of this center and related areas in the Zimmerman Library; this project broke ground in early 1992. An endowment fund to augment continuing program support also has been established.

Center for Academic Program Support (CAPS)

The Center for Academic Program Support, housed in the Zimmerman Library, provides no-charge educational assistance services to all undergraduate students. Services include library credit courses, workshops, and one-on-one tutoring. Drop-in labs for individual assistance in writing, chemistry, math, and physics are also provided. A special learning support services program is available for students with learning disabilities (see Appendix B).

More than 5,000 students used CAPS each year. In fall 1990, 46 percent of all freshmen used this service, which has been linked to freshman success. Evaluative studies showed that freshmen using these services had higher first- and second-semester grade point averages and were more likely to complete both semesters in their freshman year than were those students who did not participate in CAPS.[27]

Students may be referred or may choose to go to CAPS. While this program has not been aimed at any target group among the undergraduate student population, the CAPS Director said that special efforts are made to attract and respond to multicultural students. Active outreach to the ethnic-student services centers and the Minority Recruitment and Retention Program is conducted on an ongoing basis. Tutors receive training in diversity issues, and multicultural students are employed as tutors whenever possible. Utilization data reflected this focus: there was a higher ratio of multicultural students to Anglo students among CAPS users than among non-CAPS users.[28]

The CAPS Director believed that, for multicultural students, one of the strengths of this program was that service has been based solely on individual need. Students did not need to be labeled as "minority" or "at-risk" to avail themselves of the program, making the services not only more accessible but also more acceptable.

The location of this program in the library building and the library organizational structure is quite unusual in comparison with similar services on other campuses. The CAPS director reports to both the Associate Vice President, Academic Affairs, and the Dean of Libraries. Both of these individuals cited benefits of this arrangement in terms of strong ties to the academic side of the university and coordination with other library instructional roles and services. Financial support is provided through a line-item addition to the library's budget.

CAPS has given the library good visibility in the academic and student services arenas. It was the first library service mentioned by those interviewed outside the library. A recent survey of CAPS users also confirmed what many insiders suspected: students coming to the library to use CAPS make greater use of other library services than prior to this exposure.[29]

Latin American Program

UNM has special masters programs for Latin-American students in education and public administration. Coursework is conducted entirely in Spanish, and many of the students have limited proficiency in English. Special library tours in Spanish are arranged for these students, many of whom later make appointments with bilingual librarians for follow-up assistance. Library signage is bilingual and the collections in Spanish are substantial for a library of this size.

Traditional Library Services and Collections

Services to multicultural students were not identified as a major concern by librarians in reference and library instruction in the Zimmerman Library. Limited outreach efforts to the directors of the ethnic-student services occurred some years ago, but no further contact resulted from these visits. In 1991, the reference staff viewed a video program on cultural diversity and held a discussion on sensitivity. In addition, the library cosponsored a workshop on library instruction which included some attention to issues of diversity. One librarian characterized the current impetus on these issues in the library as awareness but not effort. Grant funding was obtained by one of the branch libraries to develop a library instruction component in a special program for multicultural students in engineering.

The main library reference department has been providing training to tutors and counselors from programs such as the Minority Recruitment and Retention Program. These tutors have been assisting students with library skills in their special service environments.

According to the Chicano Studies Bibliographer, who for many years also had responsibility for other ethnic studies, collections of ethnic studies materials in the general collections were uneven. Reference librarians felt that they have been improving, especially in literature. As multicultural faculty hiring has increased, collection areas have been built up in response to their interests. Allocations for ethnic studies materials have more than doubled in ten years, and other selectors have been very cooperative in acquiring material with diversity perspectives in their disciplines. Students and faculty outside of the library were more critical about the level of these resources, although most librarians interviewed had never received complaints about such weaknesses in the collection.

Recruitment

The Dean of Libraries identified attention to diversity as an important factor in library hiring, especially among the library faculty. Spanish proficiency is viewed as a desirable qualification although not a requirement for public service positions. Widespread advertising in Spanish-language publications has been used to reach Hispanic applicants. The practice of interviewing all qualified multicultural candidates in each hiring pool has been in place for several years. In 1992, the composition of the library faculty was 9.3 percent multicultural, with the figure for the multicultural staff at 30.7 percent.[30]

Budgetary Support

In 1991-92, the University of New Mexico spent approximately $350 per student on library support. The budget for the General Libraries was 5.6 percent of the instruction and general budget for the main campus of the university.[31] Within the libraries' budget, expenditures which could be identified for special programs included 3.4 percent for the Center for Academic Program Support, primarily for salaries.[32] Separate program budget figures for the Center for Southwest Research were not available, but it was estimated that 1.5 percent of the salary funds[33] and 1.7 percent of the acquisitions budget were allocated to this center.[34] Acquisitions funds allocated to ethnic studies represented 0.5 percent of the total, although purchases from other subject funds related to diversity were also made.[35]

Issues

Perceptions of Needs

The characterization of New Mexico as a multicultural state permeated most discussions with librarians about the needs of multicultural students. The Dean of Libraries spoke about a philosophy based upon the realization that UNM and its library are located in a state composed of many people from backgrounds which do not support formal education. Services have been developed with the understanding that young New Mexicans are likely to be intimidated by a large library; these people need all the help they can get. He felt that this basic approach was a de facto way of handling multicultural populations.

Reference librarians confirmed this perspective, with repeated expressions of the need to be alert to those students reluctant to ask questions and to find ways to approach them with offers of assistance. Differences in student needs in relation to the library were described in terms of prior experience in using libraries and of geographic factors such as proximity to the few large population areas in the state. The importance of the individual and his or her needs was the primary element in these conversations, addressing the needs of all students rather than multicultural students.

A few librarians were more specific in their discussion of the library's response to multicultural students. One reference librarian spoke of the paradox in the state, which is proud of its multicultural society yet not sensitive to the real differences; she found this to be a prevalent attitude in the library. Another stated that the library was becoming aware, but still needed educating on the real issues of diversity. These librarians also articulated differences among students of different ethnic backgrounds in areas such as communication style and problem-solving techniques. Some felt that these differences needed to be addressed in reference and library instruction or they may become barriers to students seeking these services.

Locus of Programming

The UNM Libraries are actively involved in consciously responding to multicultural student needs in two programs: the Center for Academic Program Support (CAPS) and the Center for Southwest Research. Individuals interviewed from both of these areas identified specific measures taken to reach multicultural students with their services, articulated variations in student needs related to cultural or ethnic background, and produced utilization figures demonstrating high levels of use by these students.

This approach was not as evident in the more traditional library services, such as reference and general library instruction. One reference librarian stated that issues of multiculturalism were addressed only in the response mode. Diversity in the student population was not seen by most as a factor in approach to reference work or design of library instruction.

The opportunity for collaboration between these specialized programs and traditional library services was mentioned by a few librarians, although formal links did not appear to exist. A new library-wide instruction committee has been established, but library instruction takes place in both CAPS and the Reference Department with little coordination. Many multicultural students, whose first in-depth contact with library resources occurs in the Center for Southwest Research, return to staff in that center for assistance in meeting general information needs. Those interviewed from both centers expressed concern regarding barriers in traditional library services which multicultural students face.

Perceptions of Library Responsiveness

Library skills were seen as an essential component for student success by those interviewed across the campus. The Center for Academic Program Support received high marks from everyone for improving this success and providing the link to the library. The Associate Vice President, Academic Affairs, talked about the library as a learning center where access to information and support was paramount. However, the Associate University Counsel said that the library was marginalized within the university structure; it has the potential to be the intersection of activity for faculty, students, and administration, but fails to capitalize upon this role.

Many interviewees outside of the library raised the issue of the low comfort level for multicultural students using the library. Students found the library to be confusing. Some were uncomfortable asking for help, although one said that librarians were friendly once he asked for assistance. The Director of Hispanic Student Services stated that the library was perceived by multicultural students to be a "white haven"; these students need to see more color in the library staff. Complaints have been received by some librarians and faculty members that librarians do not spend enough time with multicultural students. Interaction with librarians outside of the library context was identified as an area for possible improvement.

The Center for Southwest Research was seen by faculty and administrators as a focus for the library's response to multicultural issues. The strength of these collections is clearly a matter of pride for the university. However, the Director of African-American Studies asserted that fundamental change was needed for the library to become a multicultural learning center. He contended that multiculturalism is being addressed only as an appendage and only in terms of the Southwest; it should be the centerpiece for all fields of study.

Notes

1. University of New Mexico, Office of Student Outreach Services, *The University of New Mexico Preview 1991-92* (1991).

2. Richard C. Richardson and Elizabeth Fisk Skinner, *Achieving Quality and Diversity; Universities in a Multicultural Society* (New York: Macmillan, 1991), 49-50.

3. New Mexico Commission on Higher Education, *Planning for the Class of 2005: A Vision of the Future* (Santa Fe, NM, 1988).

4. New Mexico, Legislature, House Memorial 38 Task Force, *Increasing Participation and Success of Minority Students in Postsecondary Education: A Plan for Action in Response to House Memorial 38* (1 October 1991).

5. Ibid., Appendix B.

6. University of New Mexico, Planning and Policy Studies, *Selected Indicators on Students* (June 1991), 10.

7. Judy Jones, "From Scholes Hall," *Campus News* (February 1992), 1.

8. Chronicle of Higher Education, *The Almanac of Higher Education* (Chicago: University of Chicago Press, 1992), 60.

9. University of New Mexico, *Affirmative Action Plan for Minorities and Females, Volume I, April 2, 1991 to April 1, 1992* (1991), 6-8.

10. University of New Mexico, *UNM 2000 Plan* (May 1990, adopted by the Board of Regents on 8 November 1990), 4.

11. See, for example, *University of New Mexico Preview 1991-92*.

12. University of New Mexico, *Catalog, 1991-93* (1991), 9.

13. University of New Mexico, Provost's Office, *The New Mexico Plan; Areas for Potential Expansion* (June 1991).

14. University of New Mexico, Vice President for Academic Affairs and Vice President for Student Affairs, *Proposal for New Mexico Plan Funding 1991-92* (1991), and *New Mexico Plan Funded Projects 1992-93* (1992).

15. University of New Mexico, Planning and Policy Studies, *UNM Faculty: Summary Data* (January 1991).

16. University of New Mexico, Planning and Policy Studies, *Comparison of Characteristics of Four Beginning Freshman Cohorts, Fall 1983 through Fall 1991* (October 1991).

17. Ibid.

18. University of New Mexico, Planning and Policy Studies, *Selected Indicators on Students*, 46.

19. University of New Mexico, General Library, *UNM General Library Handbook for Faculty* (1991).

20. University of New Mexico, *Detail Operating Budget Plans, 1991-92; Main Campus: Instruction & General* (1991), 45.

21. Robert Migneault, *Summary Reallocation Recommendations* (January 1991) and *Review of the UNM General Library* (December 1991).

22. University of New Mexico, *UNM 2000 Plan*, 23.

23. Migneault, *Review*, 8.

24. Migneault, *Summary Reallocation*, 7.

25. Rose Diaz, "Historical Redirection and the Center For Southwest Research," *History News* 45 (1990): 22-24.

26. Ibid., 22.

27. University of New Mexico, Planning and Policy Studies, *Fall 1990 Beginning Freshmen Cohort, CAPS Participants and CAPS Non-participants* (September 1991); and "Freshmen CAPS Users Earn Higher Grades, Study Shows," *New Mexico Daily Lobo*, (16 September 1991), 5.

28. Ibid.

29. University of New Mexico, General Library, Center for Academic Program Support, *CAPS User Survey*, (March 1991).

30. University of New Mexico, General Library, *ARL Salary Survey 1991* (1991).

31. University of New Mexico, *Detail Operating Budget Plans, 1991-92*, 45.

32. Ibid.

33. Ibid.

34. Communication from Linda Lewis, 18 May 1992.

35. Ibid.

8
CASE STUDY
UNIVERSITY AT ALBANY,
STATE UNIVERSITY OF NEW YORK

Background

The State University of New York at Albany is one of four university centers in the SUNY system. Its original purpose as a teachers' college was expanded in 1962 to include a baccalaureate for those students not wishing to pursue a teaching career. Doctoral programs were added, and the campus was designated a university center in 1964. By 1990, the University at Albany, as it is called, had grown to offer approximately 100 baccalaureate degrees, more than 60 masters and 28 doctoral programs in a wide variety of disciplines and professions. Full-time faculty numbered 650.[1]

The Albany campus is located in a metropolitan area with a population of 750,000. In 1992, it served 16,600 students, 4,700 in graduate programs. Sixty-five hundred students lived in residence halls in a campus setting dominated by an integrated series of thirteen academic buildings connected by a continuous roof and lower-level corridors.[2] Most undergraduates were New York State residents, and their geographic origins mirrored the population density of the state.[3]

The demographic composition of the student body changed dramatically in the 1980s. In 1982, only 7.3 percent of the undergraduate students were multicultural. By 1991, this percentage had grown to 20.9 percent, with 8.7 percent of the undergraduate student body being African American, 6.0 percent Hispanic, 6.0 percent Asian, and 0.2 percent Native American.[4] The first-year class included multicultural representation of at least 24 percent in each year after 1987, with this proportion reaching 26 percent in 1991.[5]

Faculty demographics also changed during this period, although the pace was not as striking. In 1983, the percentage of full-time faculty who were not Anglo was 5.9 percent. In 1991, 2.8 percent were African American, 3.6 percent were Hispanic, 4.8 percent were Asian, and 0.3 percent were Native American, for a total of 11.5 percent. Approximately half of these multicultural faculty were at the lower ranks of assistant professor and lecturer.[6] The composition of the professional staff in 1991 was 13.2 percent multicultural, and the classified staff was 6.2 percent.[7]

The campus response to this shift in demographics was explored through interviews with key individuals covering program descriptions and personal observations. These interviews took place during the spring of 1992.

Campus Response to Diversity

Statewide Policy Environment

The political context for issues of multiculturalism in higher education in the state of New York is quite supportive. The legislature and the governor view educational success for multicultural residents as a critical component of a healthy economy for the state.[8] Several campus administrators observed that the legislative pressure on the SUNY system during the 1980s yielded significant results in terms of direction and funding. The Dean of Undergraduate Studies remarked that the impetus for change in this area was coming from all state levels: the legislature, the state education department, and the SUNY administration, and that parallels could be found in mission statements and planning documents from all three bodies.

Two important examples of planning documents from the SUNY system illustrate the prominence of multicultural issues. *Commitment to Diversity and Pluralism*[9] is a 1990 report from the Vice Chancellor's office on university-wide activities related to the recruitment, retention and enhancement of campus climate for African-American, Asian-American, Hispanic and Native-American faculty, staff, and students. One of its most important features for this study is an eight-point strategic plan for improvements in these areas. Three of the goals are relevant here: implementation of programs to increase graduation rates, expansion of programs to ease transition from high school to college, and the introduction of a general education requirement related to multiculturalism.

SUNY 2000,[10] a 1991 report from the Board of Trustees and the chancellor laying out directions, goals, and strategies for a period of ten years, includes as a key element in its mission and goals "the broadest possible access, fully representative of all segments of the population"[11] and the priority to enhance accessibility regardless of race or ethnicity, reaching and assisting those less prepared for higher education.[12] Since access is defined to "embrace enhanced efforts at retention, and progress toward successful completion,"[13] the impetus for program development and the assessment of success go well beyond initial recruitment efforts.

Campus Mission

The most recent mission statement appeared as part of the president's message in the 1991/92 budget request for the Albany campus.[14] The goal of "educating a diverse citizenry for the 21st century" was cited as a primary concern in this document. Albany was also referred to as a model for diversity and multiculturalism in higher education for the state of New York and the nation:

> The University at Albany distinguishes itself from many institutions of higher education because of its ability to achieve academic excellence and diversity within the faculty, staff, and student body. Albany is nationally ranked in the top 10 percent of public institutions in terms of selectivity and diversity. Thus, where other campuses continue to experience an eroding base of diversity, Albany is emerging as a distinctive university that is prominent in terms of its high-quality pluralistic environment. The diversity which Albany has achieved over the past five years represents an environment that most campuses are still struggling to accomplish.[15]

This rhetoric was backed up by the appearance, as a funding priority, of multiple efforts aimed at enhancing human diversity and multiculturalism throughout the university. In the 1990 accreditation self-study, efforts demonstrating institutional commitment to increasing the proportion of multicultural students were detailed, and the investment of resources to support this commitment were evident over nearly a decade.[16]

Several campus administrators talked about the change that had occurred in the campus mission and orientation on multicultural issues. Transformation of the institution in terms of faculty and student composition, culture, curriculum, and support programs was frequently mentioned. The Director of Institutional Research said that the campus had virtually reshaped itself during the 1980s. The Senior Advisor to the President and others spoke of the importance of vision and leadership of Vincent O'Leary, the president for most of this period. Two bodies that he appointed, the Committee on Racial Concerns Across the Campus and the Coalition for a Just Community, were instrumental in providing mechanisms for many campus members to be part of the change process. The Vice President for Student Affairs, who sees multiculturalism as a defining aspect of the University at Albany, also cited the youth of the institution as a factor contributing to its ability to redefine itself.

Other campus priorities identified by those interviewed were continuing budget problems and dilemmas surrounding the balance between undergraduate education and the research agenda of the university. Both of these issues have implications for the type of change described above, as declining resources and competition among organizational values make the risk taking necessary for forward movement more difficult to achieve.

Student Recruitment

The central administration of the SUNY system has initiated several funded programs for increasing recruitment of multicultural students to its campuses. These include a position dedicated to multicultural recruitment at each of the four university centers, a SUNY Office of Student Re-

Table 8.1: Undergraduate Students
Fall 1982, 1984, 1986, 1987,

Racial/Ethnic Category	Fall 1982	Fall 1984	Fall 1986	Fall 1987
American Indian or Alaskan Native	17	21	17	16
Asian or Pacific Islander	178	261	323	335
Black, Non-Hispanic	402	569	615	701
Hispanic	224	288	341	421
White, Non-Hispanic	8,883	9,395	9,276	9,452
Non-Resident Alien[a]	129	141	121	134
Unknown	1,345	829	951	722
Total: All Undergraduates	11,178	11,504	11,644	11,781
Total: Known Minority Students[b]	821	1,139	1,296	1,473
Percent Minority	7.3%	9.9%	11.1%	12.5%

Source: State University of New York, University at Albany, Office of Institutional Research, *Undergraduate, Graduate and All Students by Racial/Ethnic Origin, Fall 1982, 1984, 1986, 1987, 1988, 1989, 1990, 1991* (January 1992).

cruitment in New York City, and support for statewide networks and conferences.

At the University at Albany, an associate director for multicultural admissions was appointed in 1988. He is supported with campus funding for one support-staff member, one graduate assistant, and a staff of student assistants.

Four avenues for admission to the university exist for multicultural students. Approximately 80 multicultural stu-

By Racial/Ethnic Origin
1988, 1989, 1990, 1991

Fall 1988	Fall 1989	Fall 1990	Fall 1991	Percent Distributions Fall 1990	Fall 1991
16	21	15	20	0.1%	0.2%
402	464	560	709	4.5	6.0
856	943	986	1,041	7.9	8.7
513	588	652	713	5.2	6.0
8,761	8,455	8,163	8,203	65.5	68.9
128	113	83	97	0.7	0.8
<u>1,388</u>	<u>1,252</u>	<u>2,000</u>	<u>1,130</u>	<u>16.1</u>	<u>9.5</u>
12,064	11,836	12,459	11,913	100.0	100.1[c]
1,787	2,016	2,213	2,483		
14.8%	17.0%	17.8%	20.8%		

[a] Includes *all* non-U.S. citizens, regardless of race/ethnic origin.
[b] Excludes non-resident aliens.
[c] Discrepancy of total due to rounding off of percentages.

dents were enrolled in 1991 through the traditional admissions program. Competition for these students, many of whom were extremely well qualified, was very stiff. Another 160 students of color enrolled through the Equal Opportunities Program (EOP), which was designed for educationally and economically disadvantaged students of any race. The Multicultural Recruitment Program attracted 160 students whose qualifications fell below the traditional admissions criteria but who did not qualify for EOP. The

Associate Director, Multicultural Admissions asserted that many of these students were fully qualified for admission at other top universities. Finally, approximately 110 multicultural students entered through the talented student programs, which permit academic departments individually to admit students with special talents in athletics, music, performing arts, etc.

Recruitment for multicultural students in all of these categories was competitive due to the pressures in many colleges and universities to diversify their student bodies. Important components of this admissions program were an aggressive group of student or peer recruiters, an active on-campus tour program coordinated with student organizations, and collaboration with high schools in New York City and other urban areas in the state.

Faculty and Staff Recruitment

According to the Senior Advisor to the President, more than half of the women and people of color on the faculty in 1992 were appointed within the previous six years. Many of these came through the Target of Opportunity Program, which identifies and appoints individuals with special qualifications without the traditional search. However, the severe impact of budget problems on faculty hiring had made progress difficult; although Albany used to add fifty to sixty new faculty each year, in 1992 they were planning on adding twelve. Five of these appointments would be through the Target of Opportunity Program, two with funding from the SUNY system, and three taken from available positions before approvals were given for departmental searches.

Table 8.2: Full-Time Faculty By Race/Ethnic Origin and Rank For Fall 1991

	White	Black	Hispanic	Asian	Native American	Total
Disting. Professor	15	0	0	0	0	15
Professor	211	5	4	11	1	232
Associate Professor	215	2	7	9	1	234
Assistant Professor	103	7	9	11	0	130
Lecturer	23	4	3	0	0	30
Total	567	18	23	31	2	641

With A Percentage Comparison of Fall 1983, 1987, 1990, 1991
(Percent Minority)

	1983	1987	1990	1991
Distinguished Professor			0.0	0.0
Professor	5.7	7.3	8.1	9.1
Associate Professor	6.9	7.6	7.6	8.1
Assistant Professor	6.8	10.5	17.6	20.8
Lecturer	16.1	20.0	15.6	23.3
Total	5.9	8.6	10.1	11.5

Note: Does not include faculty with Non-Resident Alien status.
Source: State University of New York, University at Albany, Affirmative Action Office, *Affirmative Action Plan, 1992* (November 1991).

The Senior Advisor to the President characterized the climate faced by new multicultural faculty, most of whom enter at the junior level, as mixed at best. Some departments have made progress, and the numbers of faculty of color or those for whom diversity is a major issue are large enough to provide a welcoming environment. More often, these individuals were breaking new ground. Several of those interviewed talked of racism, sometimes not subtle, as a pervasive problem confronting faculty of color; lack of mentoring, areas of non-traditional research, the amount of time spent with students, and other issues related to tenure were barriers to retaining many of these people.

Searches for professional staff are subjected to the same requirements and priorities as faculty searches. The Senior Advisor to the President felt that this segment of the staff was diversifying at a fairly heartening rate, although some attrition occurred because people missed the larger ethnic communities from which they had come. Hiring of classified staff is controlled by the New York Civil Service System, which allows only the three most qualified candidates to be considered for any position. Most hiring in these positions continues to be of Anglo individuals.

Student Support Services

A major change in approach to student support services took place in 1989, when the academic support programs previously available only to EOP students were expanded to accommodate all students. The Director of Institutional Research, who was involved in the studies of student success and failure leading to this change, stated that they believed that many students were at risk in at least one area, regardless of their race, ethnicity, or academic standing.

Academic Support Services supported seven programs. Programs open to all students free of charge included the study groups providing facilitated support for eighteen *killer courses*, the University Tutors program, in which advanced students receive course credit for their work in supporting students in these same courses, an early academic warning system, a faculty mentor program, and study skills workshops taught by university faculty in areas such as time management, textbook mastery, learning from lecture, and exam strategies. Referrals to trained independent tutors were also made for students needing additional individualized attention, at a minimal charge. Approximately 500 students participate in these programs each year.

The traditional EOP support consisted of a six-week residential summer program followed by developmental courses as needed. The Associate Dean for Academic Support Services claimed that Albany had one of the highest graduation rates for EOP students in the country, with 44 percent of the 1986 entering class already graduated by 1992 and another 4-5 percent expected to graduate within the next year. In 1992, there were 850 EOP students on campus.

Support services were also offered by the Multicultural Student Services Office. This program provided personal and academic support for students of color. It grew out of student demonstrations in 1982 which, among other things, demanded services for students of color who were not EOP students. This office operated a network of peer advisors, provided general orientation to multicultural students, and supported tutoring through a special program for students in science, engineering and technology.

Library involvement in these programs has been limited to the EOP summer program and developmental courses, both of which have a library tour and instruction component. Study skills tapes were available in the library's Interactive Media Center, and Academic Support Services staff and tutors referred students to library services such as the research partnership and reference desk.

Curriculum and Pedagogy

In 1989, the University Senate passed a resolution making a human diversity requirement part of the general education requirements for all undergraduates entering in Fall 1990 and thereafter.[17] This requirement now reads:

A course shall be considered for designation as "Human Diversity Requirement" by the Curriculum Committee, subject to Undergraduate Academic Council Approval, under the following criteria:

1. They should relate directly to contemporary United States experiences of students or contain components that compare, on a fairly regular basis, aspects of other cultures to those experiences.
2. They should compare and relate aspects of racial and/or ethnic diversity, including gender-related concerns, to the topic of the course. In this context, the terms "racial" and "ethnic" may include groups of self- and/or societally-defined on such bases as nationality, religion, etc.
3. They should provide substantial knowledge of diversity as expressed through sociopolitical, ideological, aesthetic, or other aspects of human endeavor. It is not a requirement or expectation that the content will focus on controversy or those aspects that result in conflict with other persons, groups, or cultures; see however, the next criterion.

4. They should provide sufficient knowledge to permit the student to understand better the sources and manifestations of controversy and conflicts in cultural values arising from human diversity.

5. Opportunities for student writing and discussion are central to the objectives of the program. Courses should include at least one writing component. For discussions to be effective, classes of sixty or more students should require discussion sections, breakout sessions, in-class groups or comparable mechanisms permitting discussions within groups of twenty students.

6. Courses should focus on the theories, histories, dynamics, mechanisms, and results of human and social diversity, drawing on the experience of specific groups to illustrate those principles. Thus, whatever specific cultural heritages the students study should be placed in the larger context of cultural diversity.

This initiative was promoted by the president, and according to the Dean of Undergraduate Studies, was approved rather quietly although acceptance among the faculty has been varied. Many existing courses were approved for this requirement, and others have been added. This has added a substantial burden to faculty teaching in related fields.

Discussions among the faculty teaching the diversity courses centered on the need for the courses to become central, rather than marginalized within their departments. Recognition for this work has been an issue. One faculty member asserted that cross-cultural and interdisciplinary issues are at the frontiers of many disciplines; he was not abandoning the mainstream to develop this expertise but breaking new ground.

In addition, many of these faculty asserted that courses needed to be restructured to incorporate diversity into the core curriculum. The Dean of Undergraduate Studies felt that diversity was entering the mainstream through faculty who were already moving on this issue. Reeducation will be necessary for others. They have been looking for a strategy for reaching those who might be susceptible to change.

Ethnic studies programs have long been present at Albany. Well-established departments, majors, and graduate programs exist in Africana and Afro-American Studies, Hispanic Studies, and Latin-American and Caribbean Studies.

Campus Climate

When administrators and students interviewed were asked about campus climate, the first topic mentioned was the Principles for a Just Community. These principles, originally adopted by the University at Albany on May 7, 1990, resulted from campuswide discussion and the focused work of a coalition of sixty faculty, staff, and students. In a document distributing these principles to the campus, President Swygert stated that

> Just Community transforms Albany into a living model of cross-cultural cooperation and social justice. Founded on the belief that people will unite around commonly held ideals, the Just Community has as its cornerstone a set of carefully articulated principles.[18]

These principles have been posted in every campus office and have appeared in every major campus publication. According to the Vice President for Student Affairs, these principles are ascriptive characteristics rather than determining factors, meant to define common-ground experiences and goals in cocurricular and curricular interactions, activities, and obligations (see Appendix C).

Many of those interviewed attributed these principles and the climate they have created with the success of this university in dealing with inevitable conflicts without the explosive incidents occurring on other campuses across the nation. Tensions clearly existed, but the Senior Advisor to the President asserted that racist and sexist incidents were diffused in a context of proactivity. The Vice President for Student Affairs said that apprehension existed for most incoming students of all races, many of whom came from segregated communities. Continuing training was necessary as a new class enters each year. Librarians who have regular contact with students of color heard complaints about Anglo faculty members, but they observed that the general climate seemed to be improving.

Multicultural student organizations have been very active on this campus, including a wide range of ethnically based groups as well as several prominent fraternities and sororities for students of color. The Vice President for Student Affairs characterized his relations with these organizations as partnerships rather than confrontations. Campus facilities have been used on a regular basis for social events and have become a social center for multicultural students from surrounding colleges.

Retention and Graduation

Retention and graduation rates for the University at Albany compare favorably to other public universities.[19] Seventy-nine percent of all full-time freshmen in the Fall 1988 entering class returned for the third year. The return rates for some groups of multicultural students in this class were somewhat lower, but still quite strong: 79 percent of

Table 8.3: Full-Time Freshmen Graduated or Still Enrolled, 1991

After Six Years	Minority Students	All Other Students
Entering Fall 1981	48%	69%
Entering Fall 1982	56%	70%
Entering Fall 1983	40%	69%
Entering Fall 1984	37%	69%
After Four Years		
Entering Fall 1985	44%	66%
Entering Fall 1986	45%	61%

Source: State University of New York, University at Albany, Office of Institutional Research, *Graduation Rates of Undergraduate Students* (March 21, 1991).

the traditionally admitted multicultural students returned, as did 72 percent of those entering through the Multicultural Recruitment Program and 64 percent of those in EOP.

Historically, this university has graduated two out of every three traditional first-year students and three out of every four transfer students. For the entering classes of 1985 and 1986, 47.2 percent of all students graduated in four years and 51.6 percent of all students graduated in five years. Of the Fall 1986 full-time, first-year class, 61 percent of the Anglo students had graduated or were still enrolled after four years. The proportion of multicultural students from this class who graduated or were still enrolled at this point was 45 percent.[20]

Library Response

The University Libraries, including the University Library on the main campus and a branch library for public affairs and policy on the downtown campus, have a collection of more than 1.3 million volumes as of 1991. A staff of 37.5 professional librarians and 79 support staff provide the university with an array of information support services, build and process library collections, and maintain access to many electronic information sources and interactive media materials.[21] For the fiscal year 1990/91, the University at Albany budgeted $8.4 million for its libraries.[22]

Mission and Goals

A review of library annual reports from 1986 onward indicated that the first mention of diversity occurred in 1989, following the appointment of a new dean of libraries. *University Libraries Progress 1989/90* included a prominent section on affirmative action, outlining efforts to improve representation in the library workforce to be more reflective of the student body.[23]

The five-year strategic plan written in 1990 included the following as one of seven goals:

> Increase the diversity of the library staff through active affirmative action recruitment. Create an environment that encourages accomplishment, assists staff to be successful, and facilitates the retention of a diverse staff.[24]

Action steps related to this goal included increasing opportunities to recruit and hire a diverse staff, supporting the work of the University Libraries Diversity Committee, developing an internship program for multicultural students interested in librarianship, and creating a new position of multicultural services librarian.[25] In addition, a section on student diversity and diversity of demand indicated awareness of the potential impact of the increasing diversity of the student body upon library programs and services.[26]

The Dean of Libraries indicated in her interview that she viewed diversity as a major issue on campus, a high priority for the library, and a pressing concern for her personally. The Assistant Director and others spoke of the director's leadership and influence on these issues, particularly in recruitment. However, though all other librarians interviewed identified diversity as an issue for the campus as a whole, all but one discussed the impact on the library only after a specific probing question.

University Libraries Diversity Committee

In 1989, in response to a recommendation from the Committee on Racial Concerns Across the Campus, the Dean of Libraries established the University Libraries Diversity Committee with the charge to:

> increase diversity within the Libraries, a responsibility that includes not only encouraging the hiring of employees but also developing programs that are sensitive to diversity among the constituent groups served by the Libraries; foster an environment that will help sustain that diversity, [and] ensure that issues of diversity are addressed within the Libraries.[27]

In the three years of its existence, this committee's work has educated its members on the issues of multiculturalism and diversity. In 1990/91 and 1991/92, programming for the wider library faculty and staff included film

showings on issues of race and disability and lectures on
such topics as individual rights, classism, and political
correctness. The Assistant Director observed that the
committee had moved away from the matters of race and
ethnicity. Another librarian felt that the work of the
committee resulted in rhetoric but not real change.

Collection Development

In 1988, the Committee on Racial Concerns Across the
Campus included in its recommendations the statement that
"a review of library holdings ought to be conducted to
insure that important materials on people of color, women,
and non-Western writers are available to users."[28] This,
together with the approval of the curricular requirement for
courses in human diversity, led to the assignment of a
bibliographer to focus on collection development and
liaison to the faculty in areas of diversity.

In 1991, the diversity bibliographer published a statement on collection diversity in the University Libraries'
campus newsletter. In this piece, she asserted that it is the
library's "responsibility to provide resources that speak to
the new pluralism on campus," and that the library "con-
tributes to a climate of enlightened consciousness by
acquiring materials that both strengthen and broaden the
concept of pluralism."[29]

As the diversity curriculum was being developed, the
College of Humanities and Fine Arts received a $10,000
grant to purchase supporting videocassettes. The libraries
became involved and ultimately provided $35,000 to
purchase a core collection of books to complement these
programs. The ongoing budget for diversity materials in
1992 was $13,800, or 0.5 percent of the libraries' collec-

tion budget. In addition, relevant materials were being purchased by bibliographers for the various ethnic studies programs and by others in broader areas such as literature and social sciences. Other grant opportunities and special purchases have been actively pursued.[30]

At the time of this study, most librarians agreed that they had a fairly good collection in the areas of diversity and ethnic studies. However, the increased enrollment in courses related to diversity was putting significant pressure upon the available resources. For example, one reference librarian, describing problems with research topics on African-American authors, complained that not much material existed in the collections to begin with, and it all got checked out quickly. Students were forced into writing about the same authors, because the library had good collections on the top ten but little on those who were out of the mainstream. Students could not do the same level of research that would be possible on white male authors of the same period. This type of problem also existed for such topics as events in African-American history and civil rights. Because of the lack of information in these areas, students had to do much more difficult research to get to the same point.

Multicultural Internship/Library Education Scholarship Program (MILES)

To address the serious underrepresentation of African Americans, Hispanics, Asian Americans and Native Americans in librarianship, the University Libraries and the School of Information Science and Policy have developed a preprofessional paid internship program leading to a masters degree in library and information science. The first three students, undergraduate seniors with an interest in librarianship, were admitted in September 1991.[31]

Each intern has an opportunity to work in the University Libraries in a variety of library and information management activities. Once these students successfully complete the internship program, they are eligible for a full graduate scholarship at Albany's School of Information Science and Policy.[32] Stipends for work in the libraries and support for related travel to professional conferences is provided from the libraries' budget (see Appendix C).

Library Instruction for EOP Students

Reference librarians have been actively involved in the summer EOP program for many years, providing tours and working with faculty to coordinate library exercises to teach and reinforce basic library skills. The library instruction coordinator also has provided instruction to several EOP writing classes each semester. These sessions focused on interactive group activities in using the catalog and indexes as first steps in learning the process of finding information. The reference department trained EOP tutors; this was seen as helping both the students in the program and the tutors themselves.

Recruitment

As has been established, affirmative action recruitment has been a high priority for the University Libraries. In 1989, the Dean of Libraries was successful in obtaining a faculty Target of Opportunity position for the libraries and hired an African-American social science bibliographer. This individual, recruited from a nearby campus, applied for and matched the available position, interviewed for it, and was appointed. The position was not advertised, nor were other applicants interviewed.

The library's search process has been restructured to provide for more diverse interview pools and greater accountability on affirmative action issues. However, multicultural representation among the library faculty and staff has not substantially changed over the past decade. The Dean of Libraries attributed this lack of progress to the underrepresentation of people of color in research libraries and in schools of library and information science and to the fact that many library positions have been frozen due to budget restrictions. In 1992, 6.9 percent of the library faculty positions were held by people of color. The professional staff was 16.4 percent multicultural, and the multicultural proportion of the classified staff, controlled by the New York Civil Service *rule of three*, was 7.2 percent.[33]

According to the Assistant Director, recruitment of multicultural librarians and staff members has been a major goal for the library in addressing diversity issues for three reasons: 1) the need to employ people at service desks who are other than Anglo, who will give out information, help with research, forgive fines, and act as role models and authority figures for all students; 2) the sensitivity and understanding that multicultural librarians and staff members might bring to interactions and instruction in the current campus context; and 3) the improvements in service such individuals might identify that could be made by their colleagues, who are more willing to accept input from peers than from administrators.

Budgetary Support

The University at Albany spent approximately $506 per student for library services in 1990/91 and allocated 4.3 percent of the campus operations budget to the University Libraries. Internally, this budget included one line item related to the above programs, $10,000 for the MILES interns' stipends and travel expenses. In addition, $13,800 or 0.5 percent of the library acquisitions budget was allocated to support the diversity curriculum. Another $49,000 was allocated to support various ethnic studies programs, although only a portion of this was related to American ethnic studies.[34]

Issues

Perceptions of Needs

The Dean of Libraries stated that there was a strong and pervasive view among some librarians that serving multicultural students was not any different than serving all students. The challenge was to identify individual needs and then to work to serve them. Singling out multicultural students for a special service may be a signal of the assumption of inferiority. The Dean of Libraries did not share this view entirely and was working to promote more activism. In a similar statement, the Assistant Director said that they have been trying to be more available to students of color without making assumptions. She said that the librarians needed to stay open to any special needs that could be identified without saying, "Look, you are different."

Most librarians interviewed expressed comparable views and none identified differences between Anglo students and students from other ethnic backgrounds in terms of library usage patterns, requests for information, or library needs. Variation in student needs was identified in relation to prior library experience and point in college career, but this was seen to cut across all ethnic groups. Impact on approach to reference service and library instruction was also minimal.

In a somewhat different vein, the Assistant Director said that some librarians were concerned that they were too passive on these issues, that this was part of the librarians' collective personality. They questioned whether the library should not be championing the needs of multicultural students more aggressively. The Assistant Director maintained that she was comfortable with the current approach of mainstreaming these students into general services, but suggested that this might be a complacent attitude. She felt certain that the library needed an overall improvement in services and that the librarians needed to slow down and deal with the individual student and his or her needs.

Multicultural Services Librarian

In 1990, following a description of the University of California, Santa Cruz, multicultural services librarian which appeared in a leading library journal,[35] the Dean of Libraries at Albany worked with a search committee to recruit for a similar position for the University Libraries. The concept was much the same: outreach to multicultural student groups with a focus on library instruction and reference service. Reaction among some librarians, both Anglo and African-American, was negative. They feared that this new librarian would be singled out to deal with multicultural students and that other librarians would feel no responsibility for these students. The candidate pool was not particularly strong, and the search was frozen before a candidate could be selected.

The principles in the above discussion on perception of multicultural student needs appear to have developed in large part during the period when the position was being considered. Several librarians interviewed saw the position as a political expediency and questioned its validity and substance. It is not clear whether or not the position will be pursued if resources become available, although it continues to be included in the strategic plan action steps.[36]

Outreach

The Dean of Libraries identified the need to reach out to students and to ascertain their needs for library service. However, despite the aborted initiative to recruit a multicultural services librarian, little outreach was going on at the time of this study. The Head of Reference expressed interest in a broader outreach effort to increase undergraduate student use of the library. He said that the staff and faculty needed someone out there to listen and bring back concerns.

The Assistant Director discussed a new program of active library orientation and instruction for fraternities and sororities, some of which are ethnically based. They have been trying to overcome the negative images which both librarians and these groups have of each other. The library also participated for a limited time in evening classes offered in the residence halls through a program sponsored by the dean of undergraduate studies.

The library goals for 1991/92 included an action step which read, "integrate library instructional modules into academic guidance/support programs."[37] However, both the Assistant Director and the Library Instruction Coordinator indicated that, in discussions with Academic Support Programs, it was clear that mainstreaming multicultural students was the preferred approach; the library should be as embracing as possible and focus on one-on-one instruction but should not develop special programs except those in place for EOP and international students. This perception was confirmed in the interview with the Associate Dean for Academic Support Services, in which he stated that multicultural students would be served best by improved, widely known library services for all students.

One reference librarian said that the staff had not done much to assess multicultural student needs. He said that they always have looked at these issues in terms of the problems that librarians encounter in dealing with students. From his perspective, they needed the other side: how the students perceived the library; it was important not to work from assumptions based on what librarians and administrators perceived to be the needs of multicultural students. He believed that they needed to survey the students to gauge what they felt their needs were, rather than base programs on what others observed them to be.

Sensitivity at the Reference Desk

Several reference librarians expressed the need for sensitivity training for those who work on public service desks. Complaints received by these librarians from students indicated some difficulties in interactions which led students to perceive attitude problems and even racism on the part of some librarians. The Assistant Director indicated that she had received one complaint from a graduate student charging racism. She characterized this as part of a larger problem with some librarians who were not receptive to students in general; she has been working to improve this situation for several years. She felt that this was not a matter of sensitivity to one group or another but sensitivity to student needs, whatever these needs may be.

Several librarians and library administrators asserted that the predominance of Anglo librarians and staff at service desks has formed a barrier to service for multicultural students. Poor treatment of these students which may occur for a variety of reasons often has been interpreted as racism. Some multicultural students sought out librarians of color when they needed help, which created further problems within the reference department.

Mentoring

Two librarians of color were interviewed as part of this study. Both of these individuals indicated that there were major problems with retention of multicultural faculty both on the campus and in the libraries. Although there has been support from library administration, their colleagues have not offered the same opportunities and mentoring options as for the newer Anglo librarians. The importance of this issue has been recognized by the administration and has been included in several planning documents.[38]

Perceptions of Library Responsiveness

Generally, the University Library was viewed by those interviewed across the campus as doing a good job with the available resources. As the research emphasis of the campus has developed, faculty pressure upon the libraries has increased. Several individuals indicated that this was not a students' library. This was confirmed by the two students interviewed, who said that they used the library on occasion but found it to be a confusing and uncomfortable place. The Vice President for Student Affairs stated that although many things could be done by the library to be more welcoming and attract more students, this would likely trigger faculty, who view it primarily as a research library, to object strongly.

In contrast to these statements, the Student Opinion Survey conducted by the Office of Institutional Research indicates that student satisfaction with the library was quite high. In 1988, the library received the highest satisfaction score of all university functions, with 79 percent of those responding indicating that they were satisfied or very satisfied with this service.[39] In 1991, this figure had slipped to 70 percent, but it still remained higher than many other categories.[40] No discernable variation was related to ethnicity among responses to these questions.

The Vice President said that, in regards to multicultural issues, the library was conspicuous in its silence. He was hard pressed to identify anything that would draw students of color to the library, although he said that the library could be a defining place for these students within the context of its existing agenda. However, he did not feel that there was an African-American culture that says, "The library does not represent me or is defined in a way that I am outside of it." The Director of Multicultural Student Affairs also did not feel that the library was viewed as an unreceptive place for multicultural students.

Complaints about the library received by staff and faculty members focused on issues of study space and collections but not on service. Many students complained about not being able to find materials on multicultural issues or authors, or that, when they did identify them, the materials were not on the shelves. Although the positive impact of recent special additions to the collections was noted, criticism about lack of material from small presses, third world publishers, and other sources outside of the mainstream permeated many comments.

The Dean of Undergraduate Studies viewed library skills as one of the competencies students need for success. These skills have been taught by both librarians and classroom faculty to the extent possible within existing resources. The Vice President for Student Affairs saw them as a critical element in student retention and success, and would like to see the approach for all students changed from one of orientation to one of ensuring proficiency. The Director of Multicultural Student Affairs suggested that a one-credit course on library skills would be a useful approach. The Associate Dean for Academic Support Services was less clear about the link between library skills and retention, and favored active referral to existing library services.

Notes

1. State University of New York, University at Albany, *Programs and Priorities; Assessing a Decade 1980-1990; A Self-Study Report for the Middle States Association of Colleges and Schools* (1990), 3.

2. State University of New York, University at Albany, *Undergraduate Bulletin, 1991-1992* (1991), 3.

3. State University of New York, University at Albany, *Programs and Priorities*, 3.

4. State University of New York, University at Albany, Office of Institutional Research, *Undergraduate, Graduate and All Students by Racial/Ethnic Origin, Fall 1982, 1984, 1986, 1987, 1988, 1989, 1990, 1991* (January 1992).

5. State University of New York, University at Albany, Office of Institutional Research, *First-time Freshmen Minority Representation* (1991).

6. State University of New York, University at Albany, Affirmative Action Office, *Affirmative Action Plan, 1992* (November 1991), Table 2.

7. Ibid., Tables 4, 8.

8. Richard C. Richardson and Elizabeth Fisk Skinner, *Achieving Quality and Diversity; Universities in a Multicultural Society* (New York: Macmillan, 1991), 174.

9. State University of New York, Office of the Vice Chancellor for Student Affairs and Special Programs, *Commitment to Diversity and Pluralism* (Fall 1990).

10. State University of New York, Board of Trustees and Chancellor, *SUNY 2000; A Vision for the New Century* (September 1991).

11. Ibid., 3, 5.

12. Ibid., 38.

13. Ibid., 38.

14. State University of New York, *Final Budget Request; Albany Campus* (1991-92).

15. Ibid., 31.

16. State University of New York, University at Albany, *Programs and Priorities*, 35-36, 41-45, 102.

17. State University of New York, University at Albany, *Undergraduate Bulletin*, 46-48.

18. State University of New York, University at Albany, Coalition for a Just Community, "Principles for a Just Community" (two-sided poster, 1991).

19. State University of New York, University at Albany, Office of Institutional Research, *Graduation Rates of Undergraduate Students* (March 21, 1991).

20. Ibid.

21. State University of New York, University at Albany, University Libraries, *Planning Memorandum* (December 2, 1991), 7.

22. State University of New York, University at Albany, University Libraries, *Association of Research Libraries Statistics Questionnaire, 1990-91* (1991).

23. State University of New York, University at Albany, University Libraries, *University Libraries Progress 1989/90* (1990), 2.

24. State University of New York, University at Albany, University Libraries, *Strategic Plan, 1990-1995* (1990), 10.

25. Ibid., 39.

26. Ibid., 25.

27. State University of New York, University at Albany, University Libraries, *1990/91 Annual Report, University Libraries Diversity Committee* (1991).

28. State University of New York, University at Albany, Committee on Racial Concerns Across the Campus, *Final Report* (April 25, 1988), 20.

29. State University of New York, University at Albany, University Libraries, *Library Update* (Fall 1991).

30. State University of New York, University at Albany, University Libraries, *Progress Report 1990/91; University Libraries Strategic Plan* (1991), 1.

31. State University of New York, University at Albany, University Libraries, *Planning Memorandum*, 7.

32. State University of New York, University at Albany, University Libraries, *Opportunities in Libraries and Information Science.*

33. State University of New York, University at Albany, University Libraries, *Planning Memorandum*, 6.

34. State University of New York, University at Albany, University Libraries, *Library Acquisitions Expenditures 1990/91* (1991).

35. Allan J. Dyson, "Reaching Out for Outreach; A University Library Develops a New Position to Serve the School's Multicultural Students," *American Libraries* 20 (1989): 952-954.

36. State University of New York, University at Albany, University Libraries, *University Libraries Strategic Plan; Goals and Action Steps 1991-1992* (1991), 10.

37. Ibid., 5.

38. State University of New York, University at Albany, University Libraries, *Strategic Plan, 1990-95*, 35; *Progress Report, 1990/91*, 22; *Goals and Action Steps 1991-92*, 10.

39. State University of New York, University at Albany, *Programs and Priorities*, 33.

40. State University of New York, University at Albany, Office of Institutional Research, *Percent of Albany Students Satisfied with...* (1991).

PART THREE

LIBRARIES, MULTICULTURALISM, AND CHANGE

9
LIBRARY RESPONSIVENESS
AND ADAPTATION

Introduction

The three cases presented in Part Two show that significant options are available to libraries in responding to
multicultural student needs. Choices must be made in
designing programs, allocating resources, and defining the
role of the library. In order to fully consider the foundations and ramifications of these alternatives, theoretical
constructs or models of how organizations function provide
useful tools for distinguishing among the perspectives of
these libraries. A better understanding of the way in which
organizations respond and change may improve the ability
of academic libraries to adapt to meet the needs of increasingly diverse populations.

This exploration of the responses to multicultural
students in these three libraries draws on research in
organizational responsiveness and institutional adaptation
from the fields of public administration and higher education. Academic libraries in public institutions have much in
common with other public agencies:

- they serve varied public constituencies, derive
  support from public resources, and are required to

respond to policy mandates from elected and representative bodies;
- their missions are influenced by their larger institutions and by the state policy environment; and
- their roles and functions are in part determined by
their relationships within the universities which they
serve.

Theoretical Models

To study these emerging multicultural-based programs
and the factors which prompted their development, both
organizational responsiveness within the library and
institutional change at the university level must be considered.

When researchers study responsiveness at the organizational level, most consider citizen preferences, or consumer
demand, to be the central force.[1] But in one model developed by Sharp, the tension between organizational response
based on consumer demand and organizational response
based on professional judgment of need is described. In
considering these issues in libraries, four factors need to be
taken into account to conceptualize responsiveness:

1. consumer demand;[2]
2. professional judgment of need;[3]
3. change in institutional mission and values;[4] and
4. stage of institutional adaptation to student diversity.[5]

Two different theoretical models are used in this
discussion to analyze the cases just presented: one dealing
with organizational responsiveness to multicultural students,
and the other dealing with institutional adaptation to

diversity in the student population. Although the behavior of individual librarians may also play a part in the development of these programs, this individual level of analysis was not considered in this study.

Organizational Responsiveness

In the first model, the library is considered a fairly independent program within the university, with significant autonomy in decision making with regards to programming and resource allocation. This view of responsiveness accounts for three of the four factors previously mentioned and is primarily based upon the model of organizational responsiveness, developed by Sharp[6] and Saltzstein,[7] consisting of two components: consumer demand and professional judgment of need. An element of organizational change, the importance of a university-wide mission statement, is drawn from the higher-education literature[8] to enrich the model for this setting.

In this combined model, organizational response to changes in the environment in the form of modified services may be explained by various factors which prompt the response. Organizations modify services in response to:

- a change in the mission of the larger institution of which they are a part;
- the articulated demands from the populations which they serve;
- internal professional judgment that different services are needed to meet the needs of their clientele.

The subjects of analysis are university libraries, with emphasis upon programs, services, attitudes, decisions, and resources within those libraries which relate to multicultural student needs.

Institutional Adaptation

The fourth factor in conceptualizing responsiveness is found in the second model. The library response to multicultural student needs is considered within the broader context of university efforts in the area of cultural diversity and multicultural student attainment. Utilizing Richardson and Skinner's model of institutional adaptation to student diversity, which develops a continuum of change in university approaches to access and achievement,[9] library responses to multicultural students might fall within either of two stages of adaptation, depending upon the basis for the response or the emphasis of the program. These are:

- the strategic stage, where the emphasis is on transitional measures to accommodate students with different levels of preparation, and
- the adaptive stage, which changes academic practices related to issues of learning assistance, pedagogy, and curricular support using a multicultural perspective.

This multicultural perspective addresses the individual needs of each student, taking into account varying levels of preparation, expectations and values related to higher education and mode of college attendance, without regard to race or ethnicity.

This suggests that the involvement of the library in the institutional response to multicultural student needs and the level of response within library services and programs are related to the stage of that response for the university as a whole. Here, the institutional level of analysis is applied to the library's participation and contributions.

Analysis of Organizational Responsiveness

These case studies may be reviewed in terms of the model of organizational responsiveness to assess which factors are associated with the development of academic library services that respond to the needs of multicultural students. Two of the variables considered, university mission and professional judgment of need, were present in all three cases, although their impact was apparent in varying degrees. The third variable, consumer demand, appeared in only two cases, where it took different forms and may have led to different responses.

University Mission

The presence of a university mission statement in the area of multiculturalism or multicultural student attainment served to provide a motivating framework for the responses in all three libraries. At each of the universities studied, the involvement of the state legislature played a clear role in influencing the university mission statement. Strong political statements in legislative reports and documents served to trigger responses by the university or to reinforce and support efforts already underway within the system.

These additions or changes in emphasis in university mission statements affected the libraries' planning and mission statements in different ways. At the University of California, Santa Cruz, this mission had the most influence in terms of informal pressure to improve diversity in the professional staff and begin addressing student needs. However, the formal mission statement addressing multicultural issues, first articulated by the faculty in 1982, did not appear to influence the library mission statements until 1988.

The library at the University of New Mexico was affected by the university mission in the redirection of planning documents, in the development of the Center for Southwest Research, and in the focus of the Center for Academic Program Support. However, the mission statement had not had a discernable impact upon traditional library services and collections.

At the University at Albany, the impact of the campus mission statement on library strategic planning and accountability was explicit. The increased emphasis on recruitment issues related to diversity resulted in both specific hiring decisions and the development of the multicultural internship program.

Another measure of the impact of university mission, drawn from the case study interviews, was the extent to which librarians understood multicultural issues to be part of the university mission and part of the library mission. Most librarians interviewed identified multiculturalism to be one of the major issues facing their university. However, when asked about the major concerns facing the library, only librarians at the University of California, Santa Cruz, consistently mentioned multicultural issues. After probing, University at Albany librarians did discuss the implications of the university mission in multiculturalism on the library; the University of New Mexico librarians generally attributed little relationship of these issues to the library.

Professional Judgment of Need

Professional judgment of need in the form of perception of multicultural student needs and the priority of this issue in relation to other library concerns appeared to have the greatest impact on how these libraries responded. The perception of these needs by librarians at the University of California, Santa Cruz, as different from those of Anglo students led to the professional judgment that unarticulated needs required exploration and that new services were essential.

Multicultural student needs were actively discussed, and, although not all librarians were in agreement, it was generally accepted that the needs of these students for library skills and library services were different from those of Anglo students, due to variations brought about by socioeconomic class, previous exposure to libraries and automation, communication styles, and degree of comfort in using the library. Racial barriers between multicultural students and the library and librarians were also identified by some librarians.

Outreach services formed the core of the service response to these issues on this campus, based upon the assumption that existing programming did not meet the needs of multicultural students. The emphasis on first identifying these unarticulated needs and then developing new services to meet them characterized these efforts. Student perspectives on information needs and library services were sought in a variety of settings, and programs were created to address these needs.

Perceptions of multicultural student needs on the other two campuses were based on somewhat different premises but yielded similar results. The judgment at the University of New Mexico that there were no major differences in needs attributed to multicultural students resulted in an approach emphasizing inclusion of all students in all programs. Librarians at the University of New Mexico for the most part viewed multicultural student needs in the larger framework of general student needs. Although there was some recognition that students of color were frequently reluctant to ask for assistance, this was generally seen as a behavior common to most students using the library. Most librarians interviewed did not appear to be particularly engaged in the consideration of multicultural student needs and often commented that they were unable to differentiate among the students using the libraries.

Library programs and services, whether traditional services such as reference and library instruction or special services such as academic support, were available to all students. In some cases, it was not clear whether this availability could be characterized as a multicultural perspective, which takes into account the differing needs of all students, or as an instance of attending to the needs of some groups, in this case those already using the library, at the expense of others through unawareness of their values or needs.

Outreach services were important components of the two special centers related to multicultural student needs and interests: the Center for Academic Program Support (CAPS) and the Center for Southwest Research. CAPS was particularly aggressive in targeting multicultural student groups and attracting them to the center. The approach of designing a program to meet specific student needs, marketing the program to multicultural students, and then evaluating usage patterns to make sure that the service is reaching these students was quite successful. Here, the multicultural perspective in approaching student needs, that is, looking at the individual needs irrespective of race or ethnicity, is quite evident.

In more general programs, the issue of multicultural student needs was identified by the dean as an area for further study, but little discussion of this issue with students, faculty, or staff outside of the library had taken place. The question of who does and does not use the library was not being addressed. Traditional library services were focused on those students who requested assistance. Thus, in the overall sense, evidence of attention to unarticulated needs was not found.

The prevailing view of librarians at the University at Albany was that it was not appropriate to develop special programs for multicultural students on the basis of need, and therefore the issue was approached by working to improve services for all students. The University at Albany librarians interviewed also conceived of serving multicultural students as part of the larger context of serving all students. However, in contrast with the University of New Mexico, this was a topic of active debate among these librarians. The proposal for a multicultural services librarian had raised the issue of whether services to multicultural students should be focused in one individual librarian or part of the responsibilities of all librarians.

Providing a different set of services to multicultural students was seen by some as setting these students apart and making stereotypical assumptions about their level of preparation and skill. In grappling with the issue of singling out one set of needs as more deserving of attention than another, it may be that these librarians encountered the lack of a theoretical basis for doing so within an egalitarian organization. This dilemma resulted in this case in an approach to improve service to all students in an attempt to reach this group.

Most librarians interviewed did not identify differences between Anglo students and multicultural students in terms of library usage patterns, requests for information, or library needs. However, the presence of racial barriers between students of color and Anglo librarians was noted by some.

At the same time, some librarians identified the need for outreach services to reach students who were not using the library. Although the outreach functions in the proposed multicultural services position had not been distributed to other librarians, activities with some student groups outside of the library were being developed. One librarian asserted that a survey of students of color was needed to ascertain what their needs might be and that librarians relied far too much on their own observations of student needs in forming opinions about necessary services. These factors demonstrated the beginnings of attention to the unarticulated needs of multicultural students.

Consumer Demand

Consumers in this analysis of library responsiveness were defined as all users of the academic library, including students, faculty, staff, and members of the community. Consumer demand for library resources at the three universities under study most often took the form of complaints about lack of collections. Since access to relevant library materials is the end result of most library services, this is not surprising. Demand occurred through formal complaints from student organizations, faculty, and campus groups and in informal, individual interactions with all types of users at the reference desk, and in conversations related to library resources.

The level of responsiveness to demand for collections must be considered in relation to the importance of the multicultural issues in each university context and curriculum. Certainly, balance among areas for library collection development must be achieved within available resources. Regardless of budget size, it is the responsibility of the library to support the curriculum, either directly through its on-site collections or indirectly through services such as interlibrary loan and electronic databases. As Sharp pointed out, administrators cannot be expected always to act in accordance with consumer demands and at the same time resolve problems unless it is accepted that these demands entail an appropriate course of action with respect to complex issues.[10]

Demand for library services was not as apparent, perhaps due to lack of knowledge, primarily among students, about what could be expected from libraries and librarians. As Sharp observed, sufficient levels of both needs and awareness of existing and potential services must be present before individuals will contact organizations to express a demand.[11]

Consumer demand related to multicultural students and their interests could be identified at two of the libraries. There was formalized student demand for library collections at the University of California, Santa Cruz, which led, in part, to the development of outreach services to multicultural students. The continued pressure both through demands from groups outside the library and informal individual demands at the reference desk served to keep these issues near the top of the agenda for library administration.

At the University at Albany, demand for expanded collections in a campus report and from faculty working on diversity courses affected the development of related collections and the allocation of additional resources for this purpose. Individual complaints about service also had heightened awareness of sensitivity issues at the reference desk.

The absence of consumer demand at the University of New Mexico may have been partially responsible for the lack of focus on these issues in traditional library services, but this was not clear. Interviews with some outside of the library indicated dissatisfaction with existing programs and resources, suggesting the presence of unmet needs. However, no focused demand was identified.

In summary, this three-component model of organizational responsiveness is useful in explaining certain features in these library responses to multicultural student needs. While these elements overlap in several instances and it is not always possible to separate them completely, they do provide different perspectives from which to view the development of a library service philosophy and programmatic response. These views can be sharpened when seen with a fourth component, institutional adaptation.

Analysis of Institutional Adaptation

Consideration of the case study materials in terms of the model of institutional adaptation may be used to explore how the pattern of library responsiveness is related to the institution's responses to diversity. In two cases, although characterization of the universities' efforts required more than one stage, the response in the libraries was closely aligned with the stage of the university response. In the third case, the stage of university response was clearer, but the placement of the library response within this continuum was not entirely consistent with the stage of response at the university level.

University of California, Santa Cruz

During the period of time under study, the University of California, Santa Cruz, was focused on multicultural issues, and this focus was clearly reflected in the library. Faculty recruitment efforts, curricular requirements and perspectives, and student support programs were all elements of this focus. The library was actively involved in the first two areas within the scope of traditional library activities and in the last as part of wider campus programs.

The stage of institutional adaptation on this campus might be characterized in Richardson and Skinner's terms as both strategic and adaptive. This is not surprising, since the development of responses to diversity is often not sequential and more than one form usually exists on a campus at any one time.[12] Although support programs for all students were imbedded in the college structure across the university, specialized learning assistance, academic program support, and student services were focused on multicultural students. This approach falls within the strategic stage, where multicultural students are targeted for interventions that will help them become better suited for the university environment and to make the institution less difficult for them to negotiate.

The active involvement of the multicultural services librarian in the academic support programs for targeted students may be viewed as part of the strategic-stage response. Library instruction and library skills were incorporated into summer transitional programs for entering multicultural students, academic support programs for continuing students, and mentoring programs for advanced students.

In the area of curriculum and pedagogy, the approach of this campus to multiculturalism more clearly relates to the adaptive stage. The long-standing presence of an ethnic studies requirement for all students and the shift to multicultural perspectives in many mainstream courses, including the college core courses required of all first-year students, served at least to introduce these issues to all students.

Library responses related to curriculum and pedagogy, where the university would be placed at the adaptive stage, are consistent with this part of the model. Collections and reference strategies were changed, adapting to new pressures to supply information on topics generated by student assignments that reflect a curricular focus on multicultural perspectives. Librarians modified their reference interaction techniques and library instruction methods to better meet the varying communication and learning styles found in a diverse student body. These changes appeared to affect all students using library services.

University of New Mexico

The University of New Mexico also had program elements which fell into both the strategic stage and the adaptive stage in terms of adaptation to student diversity. Few programs, with the exception of the ethnic student services centers, were targeted solely at multicultural students. Student assessment was a key element in the admissions process, and support programs were in place to assist all students in need of additional preparation. The CAPS program is an example within the library which fits this approach of designing services to meet individual needs and making them available to all students, regardless of race or ethnicity. These factors clearly meet Richardson and Skinner's criteria for the adaptive stage.

However, the crucial element in the adaptive stage of faculty involvement in changing academic practices appeared to be limited on this campus. Little impact on curricular requirements or change in perspectives in courses was noted outside of the ethnic studies programs, although an ethnic studies requirement was under discussion. The slower movement of the campus toward the adaptive stage in areas of curricular change and pedagogy resulted in less impact on the library in terms of general collection development.

University at Albany, State University of New York

Of the three universities studied, the University at Albany probably came closest to full realization of the adaptive stage as described in this model. Support programs were provided according to student need rather than race and ethnicity. The university faculty had become involved in changing academic practices and the curriculum, and the institution had taken major steps to redefine itself within a multicultural context.

The adoption of a set of commonly held principles and ideals for functioning as a university community in a multicultural environment served to set a standard for interactions and involvement which transcends the issues of race and ethnicity. Strong leadership and focused strategic planning initiatives moved this campus forward in diversifying the student body, the faculty, and the administration despite limited resources and opportunities for growth.

The impact of these changes on library programs and services and the relationship between the stages of campus adaptation and library adaptation were uneven. In the case of curricular change, the collection development department responded by integrating both specific responsibility for diversity programs and broader multicultural perspectives in disciplines such as social science and literature into the bibliographers' assignments. These changes, together with the resources provided to support them, had begun to shift the emphasis of the library's collections in ways that increased the ability of users to meet their research needs.

The involvement of the library in the changes in the academic support programs was less evident. The long-standing library intervention for EOP students, which was based upon their need for transitional support in advance of beginning college work, had not been mainstreamed in the same way as the academic support programs. In fact, library involvement in this area was quite limited.

Librarians' perceptions of the needs of multicultural students led to approaches and services which focused on the individual needs of each student regardless of race or ethnicity. However, these individual needs were not clearly articulated or differentiated so that both the users and the librarians could see that accommodations in services and programs were available. Although there was discussion of these issues, the emphasis was still to a large extent on changing the students to perform within the system rather than changing the library practices to better meet the student needs.

Other elements within the library's programs were closely allied with campus efforts. Cultural awareness and training programs were present, and strategic planning documents reflected the campus priorities in this area. Recruitment strategies moved beyond expanding candidate pools to the development of an internship program designed to increase the number of students from underrepresented ethnic and racial groups entering the profession of librarianship.

Comparisons Among Responses

The clearest link between stage of university adaptation and stage of library adaptation in these libraries was in the area of curricular change. Since library collection development policies have curricular program support as a primary foundation, this is not surprising. In these three cases, the strongest efforts in developing multicultural perspectives in the libraries' general collections and accompanying reference strategies in providing access to this information were found in the two institutions where comprehensive curricular change was occurring. At the University of New Mexico, where a related core requirement did not yet exist and where less progress had been made in developing multicultural perspectives in the mainstream curriculum, the demand was not as great in traditional library services. Collection development and reference efforts related to diversity were primarily focused in special centers with barriers remaining in the general collections and services.

The other area where congruent approaches in the university and the library might be expected is in the characterization of multicultural student needs. Here, the perceptions of needs and the development of responses to meet them in the library were consistent with approaches in other parts of the campus at the University of California, Santa Cruz, and in the Center for Academic Program Support at the University of New Mexico. The slower rate of change at New Mexico in the area of curricular development may have limited the impact of the campus perspective on multicultural student needs in the rest of the library.

At the University at Albany, there was some discrepancy between the campus perspective on multicultural student needs and the perspective found in the library. On the surface these appeared to be the same, with services part of an overall commitment to all students rather than an intervention to accommodate a special clientele. However, the underlying emphasis of Richardson and Skinner's multicultural perspective on recognizing and addressing individual differences in areas such as levels of preparation, expectations and values related to higher education and mode of college attendance, without regard to race or ethnicity, was not apparent.

In summary, this model of institutional adaptation to student diversity is useful in understanding the relationship of library responsiveness to the university's response to diversity. The explanatory power of the model in these three cases was found to be stronger in the area of curricular change than in the perspective on multicultural student needs, but the consideration of the library response in the broader institutional context is useful in both instances. When used in conjunction with the three other factors in the conceptualization of responsiveness, a more focused picture of the areas of progress and stagnation can be seen at each campus.

Additional Comparative Factors

Two elements of variation among the three case studies which have not been discussed in the context of the two theoretical models merit further examination. These factors, resources and representation, may explain some of the differences in responsiveness to multicultural student needs.

Resources

A wide variation in the level of funding for library operations, services, and collections in terms of expenditures per student was found on these three campuses, as Table 9.1 indicates. Some of this range can be explained by the size of the campus and the economies of scale which can be achieved when serving larger numbers of students. However, the fact that during the period of study, the total budget at the University of New Mexico was equivalent to that at the University at Albany and the per-student expenditure ratio was less than half that at the University of California, Santa Cruz, cannot be entirely attributed to this difference. The Dean of Libraries at UNM observed that both the Library and the University were underfunded in comparison with peer institutions in other states, due to the relative lack of resources in the state of New Mexico.

Table 9.1: Annual Library Funding, 1991/92

	Budget (in millions)	Student Enrollment	Per-Student Funding
UCSC	$6.9	10,100	$683
UNM	$8.4	24,000	$350
SUNY-A	$8.4	16,600	$506

Source: Data in this table are derived from multiple sources cited in the case studies.

The impact of this resource constraint on responsiveness at the University of New Mexico took several forms. First, it may have been part of the reason that reference librarians and others in traditional library service roles focused primarily on those students who requested services rather than on outreach services to identify those not using the library. Keeping up with the demand coming through the door may have been all that was possible within the resources available. In addition, the ability to dedicate a position to outreach services as found at the University of California, Santa Cruz, and as seriously considered at the University at Albany may not have been feasible.

Most of the efforts to respond to multicultural student needs described in these three libraries were undertaken within existing library budgets. At the University of California, Santa Cruz, services were developed through the redefinition of a professional position. Collection funds, under severe pressure in all libraries due to spiraling inflation in the publishing field, were diverted to diversity-related purchasing in varying degrees in all three cases. The related resource trade-off issues were openly addressed in the interviews at UC Santa Cruz but did not come up at the other campuses.

The use of multicultural issues as an opportunity in the search for additional funding was most prominent at the University of New Mexico, where major capital support was obtained for the expansion of the Center for Southwest Research. On the other two campuses, small endowments and grants had been acquired for collection additions related to diversity.

The fact that priorities for services and collections were realigned within existing resources suggests that responsiveness to multicultural student needs in these three cases was for the most part due to a redefinition of the organizational mission. The proliferation of programs to build the scope of the resources and operations allocated to the libraries did not appear to be an overriding motivation.

Representation

Recruitment goals for increasing diversity in the library workforce, particularly at the level of professional librarian, were present in all three libraries. This was part of the larger institutional efforts as delineated above, but it was also described by some librarians as important in making multicultural students more comfortable in the library and, in one case, in making changes in services which would make the library more responsive to multicultural students. The latter two reasons for recruiting librarians of color fit the classic tenets of representative bureaucracy, wherein such organizations employ members of underrepresented groups and expect these individuals to use their influence to represent the interests of these groups, so that the organizations will become more responsive to their needs.[13]

The three libraries studied have had varying degrees of success in their recruitment efforts. As one library administrator pointed out, the limited availability of librarians from diverse racial and ethnic backgrounds prepared at the masters level is a problem. In 1991, the American Library Association reported that 12.3 percent of the 23,000 academic and public librarians in the United States were identified as from racial or ethnic backgrounds other than Anglo. In academic libraries, 14.5 percent of the entry-level positions were held by librarians from underrepresented groups.[14] Table 9.2 indicates that two of the three cases fell short of these targets.

Table 9.2: Professional Library Workforce Composition, 1991

	Number of Librarians	Number from Under-represented Groups	Percentage from Under-represented Groups
UCSC	32	4	13%
UNM	43.5	5	11%
SUNY-A	37.5	2.6	7%

Source: Data in this table are derived from multiple sources cited in the case studies.

In 1991, the University of California, Santa Cruz, came the closest to the availability figures for the profession at large. However, half of the targeted hiring represented in these figures took place within three months of the case study period. The former multicultural services librarian on this campus proved to be an effective advocate for the students and lobbied for library attention to their needs; this was one of the stated responsibilities of her position. The evidence that other librarians of color at UCSC took on this role was less clear.

Perhaps the most important endeavor identified in this area was the internship program at the University at Albany, which was aimed specifically at increasing the availability of librarians from diverse racial and ethnic backgrounds in the national workforce.

Summary Findings

In the first model, the view of organizational responsiveness from within the library, professional judgment of need emerged as an overriding factor in affecting the forms of response. Librarians' perceptions of multicultural student needs were directly linked to the services they chose either to develop or to leave unchanged. The university mission was important in providing the context for this response, but it was not enough in itself to move one library beyond the planning stage. Consumer demand, both formal and informal, provided greater pressure on these libraries to make changes in collections and, in one case, in service delivery.

In the second model, the library's response was viewed as part of the institutional adaptation of the university to diversity in the student population. The prominence of multicultural issues in broad-based curricular change resulted in new demands on two libraries. The need for change in the area of programmatic support was very powerful, since it related directly to an important component of the academic library's central mission. The perspective on needs of multicultural students was important at this level as well, showing evidence of some relationship between the characterization of these needs at the campus level and the manner in which they were defined within the library.

The additional factor of resource constraints suggested a possible explanation for some of the differences in responsiveness among these libraries, although this factor alone was not compelling.

Notes

1. See, for example, Paul D. Schumaker, "Policy Responsiveness to Protest-Group Demands," *Journal of Politics* 37 (1975): 488-521; and Sidney Verba and Norman Nie, *Participation in America* (New York: Harper and Row, 1972).

2. Elaine B. Sharp, "Responsiveness in Urban Service Delivery," *Administration and Society* 13 (1981): 33-50; Schumaker, 494; and Verba and Nie, 300.

3. Grace Hall Saltzstein, "Conceptualizing Bureaucratic Responsiveness," *Administration and Society* 17 (1985): 283-306; and Sharp, 33-50.

4. Daryl G. Smith, *The Challenge of Diversity: Involvement or Alienation in the Academy?* Report No. 5 (Washington, DC: School of Education and Human Development, George Washington University, 1989), 58.

5. Richard C. Richardson and Elizabeth Fisk Skinner, *Achieving Quality and Diversity; Universities in a Multicultural Society* (New York: Macmillan, 1991), 11-14.

6. Sharp, 33-50.

7. Saltzstein, 283-306.

8. Smith, 38.

9. Richardson and Skinner, 11-14.

10. Sharp, 45.

11. Elaine B. Sharp, *Citizen Demand-Making in the Urban Context* ([Tuscaloosa:] University of Alabama Press, 1986), 12.

12. Arthur Levine, "The Meaning of Diversity," *Change* 23 (1991): 4-5.

13. For example, see Samuel Krislov, *Representative Bureaucracy* (Englewood Cliffs, NJ: Prentice-Hall, 1974), 64-66; Frank Marini, ed. *Toward a New Public Administration* (Novato, CA: Chandler, 1970); and Grace Hall Saltzstein, "Representative Bureaucracy and Bureaucratic Responsibility: Problems and Prospects," *Administration and Society* 10 (1979): 464-475.

14. American Library Association, Office for Library Personnel Resources, *Academic and Public Librarians: Data by Race, Ethnicity & Sex, 1991* (Chicago: American Library Association, 1991).

10
MODELS FOR CHANGE

Introduction

In order to keep pace with changing institutions and student populations, librarians must accept responsibility for developing strategies and delivering services to culturally diverse users that are both responsive to their needs and supportive of institutional goals. The libraries described here and elsewhere in the literature have made choices about how to approach multicultural student needs and develop programs and services to meet them. Although evaluation research on the utilization and success of these programs is needed to measure their effectiveness, some observations regarding these alternatives may be made. This review also suggests questions concerning user population, program design, and staff development which need to be considered.

Student Needs

At the heart of the matter of responsiveness are a series of questions regarding users and their needs. This issue centers on how each library views the population of students upon which it should concentrate its primary

193

efforts. Is this group made up of those students using the service or those, identified or unidentified, who need the service? Are these needs defined within the constraints of the services available, or are services designed to meet changing needs? Do institutional directions and resource issues influence the decisions in these matters?

Librarians' Perceptions of Needs

The literature on academic library services for multicultural students indicates that responsiveness based upon professional judgment of need by librarians is an important impetus in the development of library programs for multicultural students. Statements regarding the importance of library use for multicultural student success, the low numbers of multicultural students using the libraries, and the responsibility of librarians to develop effective services in a multicultural environment appear in many of these articles.[1]

The analysis of the three case studies suggests that librarians' perceptions of need are a critical factor in shaping the library's service response to multicultural students. If the institutional environment is supportive of targeting multicultural students for special services, as was found at the University of California, Santa Cruz, the philosophical problems with singling out a segment of the population for specific treatment may be set aside, at least for a time, to identify needs and develop relevant responses.

Categorization of student needs by racial or ethnic group may create problems because assumptions must be made which oversimplify the issues and blur individual differences related to ability, background, and learning style. On the other hand, services developed for the general population often fail to address important differences in these basic areas. Ideally, these new responses would be institutionalized later by incorporating them into the general service programs as part of a broader spectrum of approaches to meet the varying needs of all students.

The embryonic approach to multicultural student needs in the library at the University at Albany, which aspires to address these needs through the improvement of services to all students, entirely avoids the risk inherent in categorization by racial or ethnic group. However, unless the barriers faced by multicultural students functioning within educational systems designed by and for the dominant culture are recognized, this may result in no more than a continuation of the status quo. To be truly responsive to the needs of students of color as well as those of all students at the individual level, a fundamental change in library service programs still may be required.

The Multicultural Perspective

To reach the multicultural perspective described by Richardson and Skinner, the library must first examine its users, its potential users, and its services to determine whether or not the approaches being used to deliver library services are meeting the varied individual needs of all students in the university regardless of race or ethnicity issues. Once an understanding is reached of the measure of present services to the ideal level of services, plans can be developed to meet the newly established goals. The initial formulation of services addressing the specific needs of some student groups may be necessary for the eventual development of an overall program to target individual needs without reference to group identity such as race or ethnicity. Without such a preliminary focus, the service response may run the risk of attending to the needs of those students already using the library at the expense of others within the student body, through a lack of knowledge or understanding of the needs of the non-user. When the existing library users come primarily from the dominant culture, significant discrimination to those from other backgrounds may be the result.

Focusing on the needs of students who are not using the library brings up several difficult issues. For example, in library instruction, addressing specific needs for additional support for this group may come at the expense of improving such support for all students. In some cases, it becomes necessary to assume that most students already using the library have enough skill to proceed on their own, in order to divert the librarians' attention to those who have not yet been fully introduced to the service.

How multicultural student needs are defined is also important to the consideration of these issues. Librarians may view users differently from the way users view themselves, both in terms of the importance of library skills to the educational experience and in terms of the extent to which current library services are available to meet existing needs. In some instances, the approach of changing users to fit librarians' perceptions and services appeared to be preferred to changing services to accommodate user demand or need. While some adjustment of student patterns of library use is certainly part of the educational process, librarians also need to question the design of library services and operations in light of varied student needs, so that there may be some meeting on middle ground. The greatest danger lies in the intransigence of any side approaching these issues.

Programs Designed for Multicultural Students

Library services and programs designed for multicultural students are described in the literature and exist in two of the institutions included in this study. In addition to variations in the content of the programs, a primary difference among these programs is the extent to which they are limited to students of color or to a particular segment of this targeted population.

Outreach

As described above, the library at the University of California, Santa Cruz, has developed outreach services aimed specifically at multicultural students to increase the use of the library by students of color. Active involvement of a librarian in campuswide learning assistance activities for multicultural students is a major element in these outreach services. Library instruction has become an important component in many campus support activities for multicultural students, including a mentorship program where thirty upper-division students receive weekly coaching on research skills and projects.

By focusing on the needs of these students and working with them outside of the library environment, the credibility of the library as an important tool in the college experience is established. This work has also enabled the library to identify barriers to library services for multicultural students and areas where general services required adaptation. The raising of awareness of the needs of these students among the library staff has also improved the responsiveness these students experience when they use library services.

Individualized Approaches

Within the larger library system at the University of New Mexico, the Center for Academic Program Support provides a good model for an approach which considers individual needs of students without differentiating among them by race or ethnicity while, at the same time, ensuring that the needs of multicultural students are being met and that the barriers to service which many of them may encounter are being addressed. The outreach strategies, staff training programs, and evaluation techniques which focus on the needs of multicultural students are important factors in the ongoing development of these services, although one of the program strengths for participating students is that they do not have to be labeled multicultural in order to qualify for the support which this program provides. In this case, the elements of race and ethnicity and the interplay of these factors in the educational process are recognized but do not form the primary basis for program development based upon categorization of student needs by group.

The peer information counseling program in the undergraduate library at the University of Michigan is another program tailored to meet the needs of multicultural students. This program was founded on the recognition that "there are often groups of students with needs so pressing and so particular that services must be targeted specifically for them, or they may not benefit from available resources."[2] Based on the assumption that one of the best resources for helping multicultural students succeed is the influence of successful multicultural students themselves, undergraduate multicultural students are employed by the library to teach information-handling and microcomputer skills, primarily at the reference desk or in the library's microcomputer learning center.

Although there are active ties between this program and other academic support programs that target multicultural students, no effort is made to limit services to these students.[3] Despite this, some of the students employed in the program challenged the implicit assumptions behind this program and so many of the others targeted for multicultural students: that these students are in need of more help or are academically less able than other students. Unfortunately, the statistical data for retention and graduation contradicts these individuals' assessment of need.

Librarians, on the other hand, valued the involvement of these students in reference service for the added approachability and credibility which their presence gave to the service for multicultural students and students in general.[4] This erosion of the service barriers may help to improve the retention and graduation levels, eventually validating these students' objections.

Instruction and Demand

The changes in library instruction methods to incorporate teaching techniques aimed at varying learning styles is an approach common to many of the programs described here and in the literature.[5] At the University of California, Santa Cruz, librarians have developed library exercises on multicultural topics for use in bibliographic instruction classes with all students (see Appendix A). Huston,[6] Hall,[7] and Fink[8] have presented new bibliographic instruction methods based upon research and experience observing varied learning styles, particularly in multicultural groups. By adapting teaching methods to respond to these learning differences, the librarian has the potential of reaching more students in general during these instructional sessions.

Another dilemma in program development relates to service capacity. Demand is such for library instruction in the classroom and at some library service desks that the prospect of an even larger user population could be daunting in the face of already overburdened resources. To address the needs of those students not using the library, choices about placement of effort and attention must be made in the context of an institutional orientation toward improving response to and performance of multicultural students. These choices could contribute to discomfort for some librarians, whose professional orientation is to provide the best possible service to every person requesting assistance.

Since the population of students able to receive services may be limited by availability of resources, introducing those who have yet to request help into this group requires that priorities be reordered to take into account social equity, a principle with growing importance at many universities and other public organizations. Institutions such as the University of California, Santa Cruz, the University of Michigan, and others have found ways to identify resources to address these needs, based on university commitments to improving responsiveness to multicultural students.

Program Integration

The way in which programs designed to address multicultural student needs are placed within the library organization may present obstacles for the integration of these new approaches into existing general library services.

When services for multicultural students are the focus of a single individual or a special center, librarians in other parts of the library may assume that the responsibility for serving these students has been delegated to others and is not their concern.

For example, at the time of this study, the services for multicultural students at the University of California, Santa Cruz, were still largely the responsibility of the multicultural services librarian. Similarly, at the University of New Mexico, the approaches and techniques for reaching and teaching multicultural students which had been developed in the Center for Academic Program Support had not been incorporated into general library programs. Failure to move such programs into the mainstream of library operations and services results in a continuation of the practice of serving multicultural students as special cases and inhibits the evolution of these services into a multicultural perspective, where support is provided to students on the basis of individual need without regard to race or ethnicity.

Diversity Positions

Professional positions with responsibilities for various types of library programs and services related to cultural diversity have been established at several institutions across the country. In 1990, five ARL libraries reported such positions.[9] Several models for these positions are presented below to illustrate contrasting approaches and issues related to these alternatives. Whether or not to focus these responsibilities in a single position has been debated in several quarters, as was noted in the case study on the University at Albany.

University of California, Santa Cruz

At the University of California, Santa Cruz, a reference position was designed to develop outreach services to reach multicultural students not using the library and to develop services responsive to their needs. The initial position description for the Multicultural Services Librarian included these duties:

> Responsible for providing leadership in library services for the campus multicultural community. Develops and coordinates an outreach program. Provides library instruction and specialized reference service in multicultural studies. Provides general reference service in the social sciences and humanities:...participates in computer reference service; prepares and presents instructional materials; selects reference materials....May be responsible for collection development in multicultural studies or another subject....[10]

As the position developed with an emphasis on academic support programs outside of the library, the active involvement of the librarian in these programs and other diversity-related activities across the campus provided the library with a high level of visibility with multicultural students. However, questions arose as to the amount of effort expended on non-library programs, especially as this began to impact upon general library activities. This position was placed in the reference department, with the intent that the individual and the new services would be integrated into departmental activities. A clearer delineation of responsibilities in both the reference department and the campus community would have been beneficial in this setting.

University of Michigan

The University of Michigan created the position of Diversity Librarian in the Graduate Library as part of their larger program of diversity efforts.[11] The duties of this position are defined in these four relatively equal allocations of time and attention:

- Provide assistance to minority graduate students and faculty in their areas of research and teaching;
- Support research and instruction in the areas of gender, race and ethnic studies;
- Support departmental and administrative diversity initiatives; and
- Monitor and coordinate library acquisitions in the areas of gender, race and ethnic studies.[12]

In its first two years, the focus of this position was to provide individualized support to multicultural graduate students and faculty and to administrators and scholars who are grappling with issues related to diversity. Faculty seminars, targeted bibliographies and packets of current readings for library and university groups involved in diversity initiatives, and library displays are examples of projects undertaken. Coordination of collection development in gender, race, and ethnic studies was also a primary concern.[13] Services to undergraduate multicultural students such as the peer information counseling program discussed earlier were handled by librarians in the undergraduate library.[14]

Michigan State University

Michigan State University proposed the new position of Diversity Librarian as part of their comprehensive plan on library diversity efforts in 1990.[15] This position is different from others in that it carries a greater emphasis on program coordination. The description of this position read:

> Reporting to the Director of Libraries, provides leadership and works cooperatively with appropriate Libraries' units and staff to develop, implement and evaluate a broad range of library programs and services to support the Michigan State University's diversity-related administrative, teaching and research activities, including efforts to recruit and retain minority faculty and students. Serves as principal liaison for diversity-related initiatives to the Office of the Provost and to the major academic units. Works cooperatively with the Libraries' development officer to generate support for diversity-related programs and services. Initiates contacts with other libraries for the purpose of shared program and resource development.[16]

When it became clear that this position was not going to be funded, a distributed structure for organizing diversity activities with existing library staff was established.

A Diversity Coordinator was appointed from the library staff with primary responsibility for the coordination of the libraries' Diversity Coordinating Committee and five focus groups dealing with library staff training and awareness, outreach, communication, resources, and research. This individual receives release time and reports to the Director of Libraries for this assignment.[17] This approach has provided for broad involvement of library staff in many diversity-related activities; in 1992, 20 percent of the libraries' staff was formally involved in the diversity focus groups with many more participating in related endeavors.[18]

Observations

While providing a focus and resource for efforts related to library services for multicultural students, the designation of a position dedicated to these activities is not without problems. Responsiveness to multicultural students may be perceived as the responsibility of this one person rather than an obligation of all library staff. As the person often in the center of library issues related to race relations, this individual may become isolated and vulnerable. Multicultural students may bypass other library service points and access the library's services through this one individual, having established working relationships with this librarian.

On the other hand, the establishment of such a position is a clear indication of commitment on the part of an academic library to multicultural students and campus diversity efforts. Libraries with such a resource have been able to move forward in significant ways in changing their services and programs to become more responsive to increasingly diverse student populations. With awareness and careful management of the pitfalls described above, this approach is viable if it is not the sole programmatic change in this area.

Collections

The increasing diversity in university and college student bodies, faculties, and curricula require academic libraries to broaden their long-standing commitment to developing collections to support varying perspectives to include information resources needed to support teaching and research from a pluralistic and global point of view. The inclusion of multicultural perspectives in mainstream disciplines as well as specialized fields such as ethnic studies dictates the need for resources that are relevant to and reflective of the cultural backgrounds of students of color.

Collection Development Policies

The manner in which the University of New Mexico's Center for Southwest Research redefined its scope to actively represent the multicultural and indigenous peoples of New Mexico provides an excellent approach for reexamining established programs and policies in the area of collection development in response to multicultural populations and interests. Although this case is related to special collections and regional history, this strategy could be expanded to address the need to provide access to a broad spectrum of opinions and views of the past and present in other fields.

Active attention to diversity-related collection development by a designated librarian working with others having responsibilities in fields such as literature, history, and the social sciences, has proven successful at the University at Albany, the University of Michigan, and others. A strong collection development policy is necessary to support the reallocation of resources to ethnic studies and diverse perspectives in general disciplines.

Special Centers

A number of large universities have established separate libraries focusing on ethnic studies or subfields such as Chicano studies and Asian-American studies. While these centers provide for intense focus on the issues, specialized

approaches to information access and acquisition of
materials from non-traditional publishing sources, and
outreach to targeted communities, they can suffer from
isolation from mainstream library programs, collections,
and resources.

Library users must seek out special centers and the
multicultural perspectives their collections represent rather
than retrieve information from multiple viewpoints in a
search of library collections on a more general topic.
Multicultural students using the center are also isolated
from other students, creating a balkanization in libraries
that is divisive for all students. These dangers affect all
areas of the library: reference, collection development,
staffing, and student use.

Perceptions of Library Resources

A continuing problem identified by librarians in this
study was the limited knowledge among students of the
resources on multicultural topics already available in
existing on-campus library collections. Perceptions among
students regarding the lack of library resources may not be
consistent with the level of support available in library
collections. However, the lack of library responsiveness in
increasing student awareness levels, student ability to locate
needed material, and student comfort in using the library
make these resources as inaccessible as if they were not
available on campus. The perception of responsiveness
therefore becomes as important as the availability of
resources.

Outreach efforts to promote accessibility to and understanding of library resources appeared to be useful in
overcoming negative perceptions about the library among

multicultural students. In two of the cases described above, library programs which included outside contact with multicultural students and related campus programs were successful in increasing the numbers of these students who used library collections.

Training and Education

Finally, training and education programs on intercultural communication and cultural sensitivity for all library staff are critical elements in programs which successfully respond to multicultural student needs. Librarians require new skills to function in a diverse environment and to adapt to the changing student population. Every library employee who comes into contact with students needs to become competent in dealing with diversity.

Libraries, such as those at the University of California, Berkeley, and the University of Michigan, that have developed comprehensive training programs for staff and incorporated diversity training into new-employee orientations, have made important progress in institutionalizing the changes in service philosophy which are essential for a multicultural environment.

Library schools must also embrace multiculturalism to attract more people of color to the profession, to ensure that all newly educated librarians have the knowledge and skills for this environment, and to provide continuing educational opportunities for the many librarians in the field facing these challenges.

Priorities

The shift in priorities in many areas outlined above represents a fundamental change for academic libraries, in line with the level of organizational change identified by many authors calling for institutional adaptation to diversity in higher education. Underlying this issue is the value conflict regarding service priorities. The library must find a way to emphasize drawing multicultural students into the library, despite pressures from other students already present and requesting service. Assumptions regarding the skills and knowledge bases of the entire student population as sufficient to assume that most can handle the library on their own may need to be made to allow librarians to focus on those needing extra assistance. While these questions are not altogether different from the long-standing debate in libraries about users and non-users, they take on special importance in a multicultural environment.

Service Philosophy

This realignment of service priorities to concentrate on the most underserved groups is consistent with some of the calls for change in the library literature.[19] However, the question of balancing competing needs and limited resources which often characterize higher education's response to disadvantaged groups[20] also comes into play. While some may view such reallocation of priorities as responsiveness to one group at the expense of another, in the case of multicultural students, the larger issue of social inequities must be addressed. A narrowly constructed conceptualization of responsiveness that accepts existing constraints can be charged with unresponsiveness in its failure to alter the overall pattern of inequity.[21]

In the longer institutional view, libraries, like their parent institutions, have lost decades of time by providing limited services to people of color, thus precipitating the inequities present in colleges and universities today. Although some perceive that services to Anglo students will be diminished by a new focus on multicultural students, in fact no general services are disappearing as a result. In the enlarged scope of services taking into account those not using the libraries and the varying individual needs of students, some new programs may not be relevant to those with skills already learned. However, for the most part there will continue to be library instruction, staff at reference points, and books on the general curriculum, as there have always been; the emphasis on multicultural student needs will not change this. In the context of the overall library budget, the proportion of resources devoted to these programs is really quite small and does not represent a threat to general operations.

Managing Change

However, the management of such change in priorities and the need to connect it to new directions in the rest of the university present challenges for libraries and library administrators. At the three universities described in the case studies, librarians struggled with making diversity issues a priority in their libraries. The shift by the universities at Albany and Santa Cruz to curricular approaches increasingly influenced by multicultural issues allowed the development of collections and services to respond to the rising numbers of requests for information on multicultural issues. However, the resource trade-offs required by this change and the need for attention to questions of sensitivity and racism in service delivery were obstacles to coordinated approaches throughout these libraries.

The choices among different approaches to the development of programs and services which are responsive to multicultural students will vary with the individual characteristics of each campus. These choices may be a function of size of the library, the student body, and the institution. Resource issues may play a part, but as has been seen in these case studies, the lack of additional or targeted resources need not be a barrier. The level of institutional commitment to multicultural issues at the university level may influence the potential for library involvement in academic support programs and other campuswide diversity efforts. The composition of the student population may affect the nature of the needs of multicultural students in a particular institution, as multiculturalism means different things in different parts of the country.

The most important choice is the commitment to make change in academic library programs to meet the needs of the increasingly diverse student population. The decisions following this commitment do not become easier, but if they are grounded in clear organizational mission and principles which value diversity, they have the chance to make a difference.

Notes

1.   Otis A. Chadley, "Addressing Cultural Diversity in Academic and Research Libraries," *College and Research Libraries* 53 (1992): 206-214; Phoebe Janes and Ellen Meltzer, "Origins and Attitudes: Training Reference Librarians for a Pluralistic World," *Reference*

Librarian no. 30 (1990): 145-155; Carla Stoffle, "A New Library for the New Undergraduate," *Library Journal* 115 (1990): 47-51; Roberto G. Trujillo and David C. Weber, "Academic Library Responses to Cultural Diversity: A Position Paper for the 1990s," *Journal of Academic Librarianship* 17 (1991): 157-161; and Janet E. Welch and R. Errol Lam, "The Library and the Pluralistic Campus in the Year 2000: Implications for Administrators." *Library Administration and Management* 5 (1991): 212-216.

2. Barbara MacAdam and Darlene P. Nichols, "Peer Information Counseling: An Academic Library Program for Minority Students," *Journal of Academic Librarianship* 15 (1989): 205.

3. Ibid., 208.

4. Ibid., 207.

5. Mary M. Huston, "May I Introduce You: Teaching Culturally Diverse End-Users Through Everyday Information Seeking Experiences," *Reference Services Review* 17 (1989): 7-11; Lizabeth Wilson, "Changing Users: Bibliographic Instruction for Whom?" in *The Evolving Educational Mission of the Library*, ed. Betsy Baker and Mary Ellen Litzinger (Chicago: Association of College and Research Libraries, 1992), 20-53; and Patrick A. Hall, "The Role of Affectivity in Instructing People of Color: Some Implications for Bibliographic Instruction," *Library Trends* 39 (1991): 316-326.

6. Huston, 7-11.

7. Hall, 316-326.

8. Deborah Fink, "Diverse Thinking: Pushing the Boundaries of Bibliographic Instruction" (paper presented at the Association of College and Research Libraries' preconference, *Cultural Diversity and Higher Education*, Atlanta, GA, 28 June 1991).

9. Chadley, 206-214.

10. University of California, Santa Cruz, University Library, "Multi-cultural Services Librarian" (10 June 1988).

11. Stoffle, 47-51; University of Michigan Library, *Point of Inter-section: The University Library and the Pluralistic Campus Community* (Ann Arbor, MI: The University of Michigan Library, 1988).

12. University of Michigan Library, *Point of Intersection II: The University Library Moves Toward Diversity* (Ann Arbor, MI: The University of Michigan Library, 1990), 14.

13. Ibid., 14-15.

14. MacAdam and Nichols, 204-209.

15. Hiram L. Davis, *MSU Idea: Library Planning Program Report* (East Lansing, MI: Michigan State University Libraries, 1990), 17.

16. Ibid.

17. Communication from Hiram L. Davis, 27 July 1993.

18. Michigan State University Libraries, *Diversity and the MSU Libraries* (East Lansing, MI: Michigan State University Libraries, 1992).

19. Rhonda Rios Kravitz, Adelia Lines, and Vivian Sykes, "Serving the Emerging Majority: Documenting Their Voices," *Library Administration and Management* 5 (1991): 184-188.

20. Michael S. McPherson, "Value Conflicts in American Higher Education," *Journal of Higher Education* 54 (1983): 266.

21. Grace Hall Saltzstein, "Conceptualizing Bureaucratic Responsive-ness," *Administration and Society* 17 (1985): 285.

11
A LIBRARY AGENDA FOR CHANGE

Introduction

For the library to be effective, all students must perceive that it is an important and accessible component of their education. To be successful in the increasingly diverse environment found on many college and university campuses, librarians must question programs and services which are based upon long-standing assumptions about students from dominant-culture backgrounds.

The emphasis on support services in the models for successful campus diversity, particularly those in the academic arena, offer the library important opportunities for becoming directly involved. In developing library services which are responsive to the needs of multicultural as well as Anglo students, the research previously cited on alienation and other barriers to success should be considered. In order to create a supportive learning environment for all students, issues of differing study patterns, communication modes, learning styles, and language proficiencies must be addressed. Emerging library programs working to create such support demonstrate the potential of academic libraries in meeting the needs of multicultural students.

As part of a larger institution facing a changing student body, librarians must seek to understand their university's or college's stage of adaptation to that population. The library can be an active participant and even a leader in developing responsive approaches to meeting student needs. This role may be influenced by the level of institutional adaptation but need not be overly constrained by slow movement elsewhere on campus. As a central unit used by most of the campus community, the library can influence issues of climate, provide exposure to diverse perspectives, and offer active support to students in their academic and personal pursuits. By setting the example for the campus, other areas of the university, from academic units to administrative units to residential units will find it easier to follow.

In any case, it is up to librarians to assess the need for library involvement and to develop the library's role. The institution's adaptation to a diverse student body has the potential to bypass the library, and resources will develop in other parts of the college or university if libraries are not proactive in delineating an active role to meet these needs.

Ways to Participate

Libraries are organizations made up of individuals capable of initiating the steps for change. If we wait for our institutions to move, the necessary changes may never occur. Each of us can make a difference if we commit ourselves to changing the libraries in which we work. The following set of challenges is offered to provide food for thought on where *you* might begin to work on this crucial agenda for change:

- *Educate yourself.*

  Develop an awareness of the issues of ethnicity, racism, and cultural pluralism as they relate to higher education. Seek to understand the experiences, cultures, and perspectives of the diverse components of your community. Examine your own prejudices—we all have them—and work to overcome these in your thinking and in your behavior.

- *Learn about your students.*

  Develop an understanding of the major multicultural groups in your student body. Find out where they are coming from and what problems they are encountering in getting their education. Recognize varying learning styles, study habits, and research interests. Be aware of rates of retention and graduation, and seek to understand the reasons for attrition.

- *Look at your library.*

  Compare the students who use the library with the students you see when you walk across the campus. Ask who is not using the library, and why not. Question your assumptions about how students view the library. Identify barriers in your programs and services which students may be encountering. Consider whether your library offers a welcoming environment to all students.

- *Analyze your collections.*

  Ask if you are doing enough to provide access to alternative materials and perspectives. Seek the assessment of multicultural students and faculty, ethnic studies specialists, and your library colleagues about the adequacy of your holdings in diversity-related research, in works written by people of color, and in multicultural perspectives in history and literature, the social sciences, and other disciplines.

- *Listen to your users.*

  Find opportunities to ask students about their experiences and problems with the library, and listen carefully to their responses. Seek out multicultural faculty and staff and engage them in discussions about the library. Be open to criticism and do not take it personally. Find ways to bring these comments and ideas back to your colleagues.

- *Be alert to interactions that might be considered racist.*

  Step back from your encounters with multicultural students and faculty. Think about the different ways in which your comments might be interpreted. Consider the cultural foundations and implications of your language, your communication style, and your assumptions.

- *Be an active voice in recruiting for diversity.*

  Serve on search committees and initiate proactive techniques whenever possible. Develop contacts through your professional colleagues and organizations. Identify potential multicultural candidates and nominate them for relevant positions. Support new colleagues as they become members of your libraries.

- *Identify others concerned with diversity and join forces.*

  Find allies in the library, on the campus, and in your professional circles. Develop projects for collaboration. Give support when others encounter obstacles.

- *Find out what other libraries are doing.*

  Attend some of the growing number of professional meetings giving attention to these issues. Keep up with the expanding literature on these topics in libraries and in higher education. Identify models which might work in your setting.

- *Study your college's or university's diversity programs.*

  Look for opportunities for library involvement. Find out if learning assistance programs offer sessions on research or library skills. Offer to become involved in a summer bridge program for new multicultural students.

- *Raise campus awareness of diversity.*

  Look for ways to use library resources to celebrate
  diversity. Mount displays on topics of cultural heritage, diverse perspectives, and multicultural leaders.
  Offer lectures, seminars, and film series to the campus at large. Develop bibliographies highlighting
  relevant library holdings. Become involved in
  campus diversity events.

- *Speak up for diversity in the library and on the campus.*

  Ensure that library goals and plans include statements on diversity. Volunteer for campuswide
  committees to make sure that issues concerning the
  total population are addressed. Get involved so that
  you and your library will help to mold the future of
  your college or university.

- *Keep working even if change is slow.*

  Recognize small advances. Think back to where you
  were last year and celebrate your achievements, no
  matter how limited. Let your colleagues know when
  you appreciate their contributions. Acknowledge
  that even two steps forward and one step back is
  progress. Do not give up.

Much of this agenda represents a significant change in
priorities for academic libraries, one that will not come
easily. As fundamental principles are challenged and the
paradigm for service shifts, librarians will need to learn
from the inevitable conflict and promote multicultural
perspectives.

Our strength lies in the centrality of our mission to the educational endeavors of our institutions, in our basic commitment to a diversity of perspectives and ideas, and in our orientation to responsive service for all members of our communities. We must put this strength to use in reshaping our libraries, our colleges, and our universities to respond to the increasingly multicultural population of our country.

APPENDIX A
UNIVERSITY OF CALIFORNIA, SANTA CRUZ

Excerpts from Job Announcement

TITLE: Multicultural Services Librarian
RANK: Assistant/Associate Librarian
POSITION AVAILABLE: September 1, 1988

Position and Responsibilities

Reporting to the Head of Reference Services:
Responsible for providing leadership in library services for the campus multicultural community. Develops and coordinates an outreach program. Provides library instruction and specialized reference service in multicultural studies. Provides general reference service in the social sciences and humanities: serves 12-15 hours a week at the Reference Desk, including weekend and evening service; participates in computer reference service; prepares and presents instructional materials; selects reference materials. Participates in library-wide activities, including administrative committees and special projects. May be responsible for collection development in multicultural studies or another subject area under the general direction of the Head of Collection Planning.

Qualifications

Required: graduate degree from an ALA-accredited library school, or equivalent training and experience; demonstrated ability to communicate with, establish ties with, and develop an intensive outreach program to the UCSC multicultural community; broad interest in the humanities and social sciences and in working with undergraduates, graduate

223

students, and faculty; ability to work at the Reference Desk, provide library instruction, and perform online searches.

The Campus

UC Santa Cruz has an active and growing multicultural community, including an ethnically diverse faculty, and organizations representing the many Afro-American, Asian American, Chicano, and Native American students on campus. The campus offers many courses focusing on ethnic groups inside and outside the U.S. and an undergraduate major in ethnic studies, as part of the American Studies Program. All undergraduates must fulfill an ethnic studies/Third World general education requirement....   6/10/88

* * * * *

Sample UCSC Library Exercises

I KNOW WHY THE CAGED BIRD SINGS

A UCSC Library Exercise

The following questions will teach you how to use some of the most important resources in the library to find readings related to the Core Course and to help your future term paper research.

MELVYL:

The UCSC library has a MELVYL online catalog for finding books by author, title or subject.

Sample searches:
You can search by title word [**f tw** caged bird sings]
You can search by exact title [**f xt** I know why the caged bird sings]
You can search by personal author [**f pa** angelou, maya]
You can search by subject [**f su** angelou, maya]
You can search by exact subject [**f xs** angelou, maya-
            biography]
Use these samples to answer the following questions.

Title Word Searching:

1. Using [f tw caged bird sings at UCSC] find the UCSC title. Give its call number _____
   On what floor is it located in the McHenry Library?_____

Author Searching:

2. Using [f pa angelou, maya at ucsc], how many books authored by her do we have at UCSC? _____

Subject Searching:

Sometimes you will not be able to find the exact book you are looking for because it is checked out, or we do not own it. But if you use the "subject headings" part of the record, you will have other options for identifying additional books on the same or similar topic.

3. Use [f su entertainers united states biography at ucsc]. What other books written by Maya Angelou are under that subject heading?

   _____

4. Using [f su maya angelou] as a subject how many books do you find in the UC system? _____

Reference Books:

MELVYL can also be helpful in finding reference material owned by the library.

5. Using [f xs afro-americans-dictionaries and encyclopedias] see how many books we own at UCSC with that exact subject heading. _
6. In the reference stacks find the call number **REF E185 .E55** (*Encyclopedia of Black America*). Check the index to see if Maya Angelou is listed. Give the page number. _____

Bibliographies:

A very helpful way of finding additional materials on one person is to find a bibliography.

Choose question 7a or 7b.

7a. In the reference "z's" find the call number **Ref Z1299 .N39 G57 1989** (*Black American Women in Literature: A Bibliography 1976 through 1987.*) Find the chapter on Maya Angelou and give the page numbers. _____

7b. Use **Ref Z1361 .N39 B67 1984** (*Black Americans in Autobiography*). How many books by Maya Angelou does it review? _____

Periodicals, Periodical Articles, Reviews, and Essays:
8. Find an interview with Maya Angelou in *Humanities Index, vol. 15* (Index Table 3). Give the title of the magazine in which it appeared. _____
Does UCSC own this magazine? _____

9. Using *In Black and White*, (Index Table 18), find the article that appeared on Maya Angelou in *Current Biography*. In what year did the title appear? _____

10. Using *Book Review Digest 1986* (Index Table A) find the date of the *N.Y. Times Book Review* of *All God's Children Need Traveling Shoes.* _____

11. Using *Book Review Index* (Index Table A), volume 1A-B, find and record the page on which the reviews of *I Know Why the Caged Bird Sings* appears. _____

12. Using the *Dictionary of Literary Biography*, (11C Index wall shelves) volume 38, find and record the page on which a bibliography appears on Maya Angelou's work. _____

[developed by Vivian Sykes]

* * * * *

SILKO'S CEREMONY

A UCSC Library Exercise

The following questions will teach you how to use some of the most important resources in the Library to find readings related to the Core Course and to help your future term paper research.

The first page shows you how to use the MELVYL Catalog to find books in the library. The second page illustrates the use of periodical indexes to find articles by subject, and the UCSC Serials List to locate journals by their titles.

1. Give the UCSC call number of a 1980 book on Leslie Marmon Silko. (MELVYL command mode: **find su silko at ucsc**, then **display**) _____

   (then **d long**) On what pages is this book's bibliography? _____

   (then consult the "call number directory" slip)
   On what floor of the library is this book located? _____

2. Find a book on native American women's literature, entitled *That's what she said.* (**f xt that's what she**), and then display its subject headings. (**d su**)

   What's the best heading for native American women? _____

   Bonus: Use this heading with the subheading—bibliography to find a 1983 bibliography of native American women authors. (**f xs..............—bibliography**)

3. Find a book on ceremonialism at the Laguna Pueblo where Silko grew up.
   (hint: if the subject search **f su laguna ceremonialism**—doesn't work, try a title word search)

   Give its call number_____and floor number_____

Do 4 or 5 or 6.

4. Find the call number of the *Handbook of North American Indians*. Find the volume number which contains a chapter on the Laguna Pueblo (and an account of various marriages of Silko's other ancestors, the Marmons, into the tribe). _____

    Since the Laguna is so close to the Navajo nation, why are they in different volumes? _____

5. Find a book of statistics on Native Americans entitled *Nations within a nation*. Table 2.17 shows the area of selected reservations. Give the areas of the Laguna and Navajo reservations.

    _____   _____

    Table 3.10 shows populations. Note the growth since 1943. Give the 1983 numbers for the two groups. _____   _____

6. By the yellow wall near Index Table 9 is *Contemporary Literary Criticism*. Find, in volume 23, the collection of long quotations on Leslie Silko. The excerpt from Jarold Ramsey's essay mentions a book of Laguna myths by Boas.
    What is the title of the Boas book? _____
    Which UC libraries have this book? _____

Periodicals, Periodical Articles, Reviews & Essays

Do 7. Do 8 or 9. Do 10 or 11.

7. UCSC periodicals are listed by title in the yellow *Serials List*. Below the title is the call number where they are shelved in the library.

    Find the call number of the journal *MELUS*. _____

    On what floor is this? _____

    You can also find journal titles in the MELVYL Catalog. (**f pe melus** then **d long**)

For what is MELUS an abbreviation? _____

Periodical Indexes

8. The Spring 1985 issue of *MELUS* has two articles on Silko. They
    are listed in the *Humanities Index* (vol. 13) on Table 3. One is
    entitled "Thinking woman and feeling man."

    What's it about? _____

9. Use the *Humanities Index* (vol. 11) on Table 3 to find an article on
    the sense of place in Silko's *Ceremony*.

    Give the title of the journal, and the date and pages of the article.

    _____

10. Use *Book Review Digest* (1977), on the low shelves near Table
    10, to find reviews of *Ceremony*.

    According to the reviewer in the *Library Journal*, on what kind of
    reservation is the novel set? _____

    Is the reviewer right? (see question 4 or 5 if you think so) _____

    Give the date and pages of the 1400 word review in *Harpers*.

    _____

11. Use *Essay and General Literature Index*, Table 2, to find a 1987
    essay on Silko, entitled "Earthly relations, carnal knowledge."

    Give the title of the book which contains it._____

    _____

    Find the UCSC call number of the book in the MELVYL Catalog

    _____   [developed by Alan Ritch]

APPENDIX B
UNIVERSITY OF NEW MEXICO

Excerpts from Library Informational Leaflets

CAPS SERVICES
Center for Academic Program Support
Zimmerman Library

The University of New Mexico General Library's Center for Academic Program Support (CAPS) provides academic support services for UNM students enrolled in courses numbered 100-499. The Center is located on the third floor of the Zimmerman Library. Services are free and students must register in person before making appointments.

The Center is open Monday-Saturday during the fall and spring semesters. Hours vary during the summer session and CAPS is closed during academic breaks. For specific hours available call 277-4560.

Center services include an individual tutoring program which includes tutoring for students with learning disabilities, math, writing, chemistry and physics labs, small-group workshops, study-skills workshops, a Supplemental Instruction program, and credit courses.

> The **individual tutorial program** is designed to provide one-to-one instruction for students in any subject at the undergraduate level except writing. A specialized tutorial program has been developed for students with learning disabilities. Appointments are needed for these services.

The **math, chemistry** and **physics labs** are designed to provide one-to-one instruction on a drop-in basis for students enrolled in math and science courses. Students may drop in at any time during lab hours. Lab services may be used to supplement instruction received during scheduled one-to-one tutoring.

The **writing lab** is a walk-in lab designed to assist students with writing assignments. Students may drop in at any time during lab hours. Tutors will help with any and all phases of the writing process. Particular attention is given to students who are working on assignments from Freshman English courses.

Small-group workshops have been developed for students enrolled in specific math, English and science courses. The workshops focus on a specific topic from the course syllabus; topics change weekly.

Study-skills workshops on topics such as note-taking, test-taking and time-management are offered each semester.

The Supplemental Instruction (SI) Program is designed to identify high-risk courses and provide a series of small-group sessions to support students enrolled in those courses. The sessions provide a chance for the students to get together to compare notes, to talk about assignments, and to test themselves. An SI leader is present at each class meeting and at each SI session to facilitate the SI activities.

Library Academic Skills Management Credit Courses are a series of three credit courses entitled "Introduction to Learning Strategies" (2 credit hours), "Introduction to Information Research Strategies" (2 credit hours), and "Research Paper Development" (1 credit hour). These courses are taught by library faculty and Center staff.

The Center also provides support services to faculty including assessment of textbook readability levels, in-class subject-area and Center information presentations, in-class study-skills presentations, and individual consultations regarding the needs of specific students. The

Learning Disabilities Services Coordinator is available to provide information concerning the needs of students with learning disabilities. In addition, the Center functions as a student referral center, referring students to such offices as Career Planning and Placement, Dean of Students, Testing Division, academic advisement centers, etc.

9/23/91

* * * * *

CENTER FOR SOUTHWEST RESEARCH
Zimmerman Library

The Special Collections Department is a major resource center for the study of the American West, including the Southwest. It is also a special care facility for archives, manuscripts, historical photographs, architectural documents, and rare books. It includes strong collections on Western Americana, New Mexicana, and Latin Americana, an architectural records collection, and a rare book room. Books, periodicals, microforms, manuscripts, photographs and other forms of material are available. While the chief obligation of the Department is to serve the students, faculty and staff of the University in support of its programs of teaching and research, it also serves local and out-of-town researchers and supports study at all levels of sophistication. The holdings of the Department are almost entirely non-circulating and are available for use in the Department about forty-five hours per week. Each unit of the department provides indepth reference assistance with that unit, and general reference assistance is available at the Coronado reference desk during the hours the department is open, Monday through Friday, 8:00 - 4:30 and Tuesday and Wednesday evenings, 6:30 - 9:30. For more information, call 277-6451. The Special Collections Department is located in the original architecturally distinctive west wing of the Zimmerman Library. Within the department are several distinct units of operation as described below.

The Clinton P. Anderson Room: Western Americana. The Clinton P. Anderson Room contains more than seven thousand books and several hundred pamphlets, reprints, and magazine editions. The core of this collection consists of the hundreds of volumes on Western Americana and Native American ethnology and history collected by Senator Clinton P. Anderson, an avid reader and scholar of the history of the American West. His donation of these books to the General Library, along with the facilities for housing them, has given the University of New Mexico one of the finest collections of its kind. Senator Anderson's donation also contains his "presidential collection" of books which includes autographs and inscriptions from his many political friends. The General Library is continually adding to the Western Americana collection through the purchase of books and through donations.

The Coronado Room: New Mexicana. The New Mexicana collection in the Coronado Room includes materials of all types dealing with the historical, political, social, and cultural development of New Mexico. Indian affairs, land grants, folklore, family history, anthropology, education, and history are important areas covered by this collection. Examples of important research materials in the Coronado Room include: copies of four major colonial archives (the Archivo General de Indias, the Archivo General de la Nacion, the Parral Archives, and the Bexar Archives), works by New Mexico authors, various censuses of New Mexico, and church records. There are also publications relating to historical research in New Mexicana including guides, inventories, bibliographies, handbooks, and dictionaries, as well as thousands of books, both fiction and non-fiction, relating to New Mexico and the Spanish borderlands. The geographical coverage of this collection includes not only the present state of New Mexico, but also those areas defined by previous jurisdictions.

The Manuscripts Collections: personal and institutional papers. Also accessible through the Coronado Room are over 500 archives and manuscript collections of institutions, organizations, well-known New Mexicans, and others who have contributed to the cultural and history of New Mexico and the Spanish borderlands. These original materials include videotapes, oral history tapes such as the Doris Duke collection, and papers, such as diaries, correspondence, and manuscripts....

The Thomas Bell Room: rare books. The Thomas Bell Room, named after UNM's first Rhodes scholar and donor of the core collection, houses over ten thousand rare books, photographs, maps, and items requiring special care and handling. A wide variety of subjects and authors are included in the rare books collection. Other materials in the Bell Room requiring the special care and environmental controls available here include pamphlets, broadsides and other printed ephemera....

The Photoarchives: photographs. The Photoarchives collection contains significant holdings related to the peoples, places, and economy of the Southwest and Latin America. Photographs are available for research and reproduction....

The John Gaw Meem Archive of Southwest Architecture: architectural materials. This archive was established in 1975 with the donation of the works of John Gaw Meem, a major Southwest architect. His collection includes drawings and perspectives, correspondence, books, periodicals, and photographs of the interior and exterior of Meem-designed buildings, and the Historical American Building Survey of the 1930s and 1940s. This material forms the basis of a continuously growing collection of architectural donations....

The University Archives: UNM records and materials. The University Archives at the University of New Mexico was established in 1985 in conjunction with planning for the University Centennial celebration in 1989. The purpose of the division is to collect, organize, preserve, and make available materials of permanent value to the University which have historical, legal, fiscal, or administrative significance. Among the many University source materials available, some of which date back to the late 1800s, are presidential correspondence, records of the Board of Regents, faculty committee minutes and reports, materials from homecoming celebrations and commencement ceremonies, architectural planning documents, and campus yearbooks. Also available are published and unpublished materials relating to the University of New Mexico, including student newspapers, class catalogs, theses and dissertations, papers of professors, and publications of the University of New Mexico Press. Materials dealing with state, local, and national history and politics can also be found in the University Archives. Besides document files, the University Archives has collections of film, tapes, and photographic materials.

Latin American and Iberian Collections. Interspersed among several of the collections described above, especially those housed in the Thomas Bell Rare Book Room and other restricted access areas, are a large and varied number of books, pamphlets, newspapers, government publications and related materials, documenting Latin American history and life from pre-Columbian times to the present. Already mentioned are the Coronado Room Spanish archival materials. In addition, the Latin American and Peninsular holdings include the following broad topics and categories: rare and unusual Mexican imprints from the eighteenth and nineteenth centuries, early Latin American travel accounts (especially of Brazil and Mexico), the history of books and printing in colonial Spanish America, contemporary Brazilian avant-garde literature and small press publications, popular graphic material from the Porfirian and revolutionary periods in Mexico, twentieth-century Latin American rural sociology, and the Spanish Civil War.

9/8/89

APPENDIX C
UNIVERSITY AT ALBANY,
STATE UNIVERSITY OF NEW YORK

Excerpts from University Informational Brochures

OPPORTUNITIES IN LIBRARY AND INFORMATION SCIENCE

What is MILES?

The Multicultural Internship/Library Education Scholarship (MILES) is a program sponsored jointly by the University at Albany's University Libraries and the School of Information Science and Policy. MILES offers underrepresented students (African American, Native American, Asian American or Hispanic) interested in a career in librarianship and information systems paid internships and graduate scholarship opportunities.

What will the program provide?

Students who are accepted into the MILES program will receive a paid pre-professional internship in the University Libraries during their last year of undergraduate study. The internship will cover two semesters and will provide the students with the opportunity to work in a variety of areas of library and information management. Students who successfully complete the internship program may apply to the School of Information Science and Policy. If accepted in the graduate school, students will be offered a full tuition scholarship.

How can the internship be beneficial to interested students?

Student interns are offered an enriched educational experience at one of the nation's top 100 research libraries. In addition to becoming involved in a broad spectrum of contemporary library and information systems operations, student interns will develop research and information management skills which assist them in all their coursework. Student interns will work with library staff to learn how research materials are selected, acquired and made accessible to users; how to use reference materials and online information retrieval; and how to use interactive media and online systems. After completing the two-semester internship program, interns should have a clear understanding of the variety of opportunities available to librarians and information managers.

What career opportunities are available?

People who can understand the information needs of individuals and who can find ways to satisfy those needs and manage the vast quantities of information in today's "information abundance world" will be in great demand in government, business and industry, and elementary, secondary, and higher education. Opportunities in libraries and information centers exist in state and federal government, school districts, colleges and universities, law, medicine, public libraries, private industry, and wherever information experts are needed. The outlook for information careers is very good across the United States and starting salaries for entry level positions are competitive.

How do you apply?

Students with a GPA of at least 2.8 may apply for the MILES Program during their junior year. Each applicant must submit a resume, current transcript, three letters of recommendation and a brief essay describing his/her interest in librarianship. Applications should be submitted to Meredith Butler, Director of Libraries, UL-123, University at Albany, State University of New York, 1400 Washington Avenue, Albany, NY 1222. Additional information about the MILES program may be obtained by calling (518) 442-3568.

* * * * *

PRINCIPLES FOR A JUST COMMUNITY

The University at Albany, State University of New York, is an academic community dedicated to the ideals of justice. A university is above all a place where intellectual life is central and where faculty, staff, and students strive together for excellence in the pursuit of knowledge. It is a particular kind of community with special purposes. Moreover, this academic community, if it is to support our broader ideals, must also be just.

There is no definitive theory of justice. The differences in these theories are to be respected. However, among all democratic theories of justice, the principles of equality and liberty are basic. These principles are no less central to a free university.

Equality is a necessary part of any university that claims to be a democratic institution. Distinctions based on irrelevant differences are ruled out. Ascriptive characteristics such as race, religion, gender, class, ethnic background, or sexual preference determine neither the value of individuals nor the legitimacy of their views. Only the merit of the individual as a participant in the life of the academic community is worthy of consideration. Bigotry in any form is antithetical to the University's ideals on intellectual, political, and moral grounds and must be challenged and rejected.

Liberty is an equally precious academic principle because the free expression of ideas is the central part of university life. To sustain the advancement and dissemination of knowledge and understanding, the University must allow the free expression of ideas, no matter how outrageous. Protecting speech in all its forms, however, does not mean condoning all ideas or actions. The University sets high standards for itself and denounces the violation of these standards in unequivocal terms. Harassment and other behavior that intrudes upon the rights of others is unacceptable and subject to action under the guidelines of the institution.

There is no guarantee that the principles of justice, once stated, are realized. The University must constantly remind itself that its mission and ethos must evolve within the context of justice. A just community is always on guard against injustice, always struggling to move closer to the ideal of justice, always asserting its dedication to justice. The assertion of justice takes its place in every part of the community: in the classroom, the lecture hall, the Library, the residence and dining hall, wherever members of the University come together. It is the responsibility of all faculty, staff and students to keep the ideals of justice uppermost in the minds of the members of the University so that they may be achieved.

May 7, 1990

SELECTED REFERENCES

Adams, Maurianne. "Cultural Inclusion in the American College Classroom." *New Directions for Teaching and Learning* no. 49 (1992): 5-17.

Allen, Mary Beth. "International Students in Academic Libraries: A User Survey." *College and Research Libraries* 54 (1993): 323-333.

Allen, Walter R. "The Color of Success: African-American College Student Outcomes at Predominantly White and Historically Black Public Colleges and Universities." *Harvard Educational Review* 62 (1992): 26-44.

Allen, Walter R., Edgar G. Epps, and Nesha Z. Haniff, eds. *College in Black and White*. Albany: State University of New York Press, 1991.

American Council on Education. *Campus Trends 1990*. Washington, DC: American Council on Education, 1990.

_____. *One-Third of a Nation; a Report of the Commission on Minority Participation in Education and American Life*. Washington, DC: American Council on Education and Education Commission of the States, 1988.

American Library Association, Office for Library Personnel Resources. *Academic and Public Librarians: Data by Race, Ethnicity & Sex, 1991*. Chicago: American Library Association, 1991.

241

Association of Research Libraries, Office of Management Studies. *Cultural Diversity Programming in ARL Libraries*, SPEC Kit #165. Washington, DC: Association of Research Libraries, 1990.

_____. "H.W. Wilson Foundation Continues Support for ARL Diversity Project" (press release). Washington, DC, April 16, 1992.

_____. *Minority Recruitment and Retention in ARL Libraries*, SPEC Kit #167. Washington, DC: Association of Research Libraries, 1990.

Astin, Alexander W. "Diversity and Multiculturalism on the Campus; How Are Students Affected?" *Change* 25 (1993): 44-49.

_____. *Minorities in American Higher Education*. San Francisco: Jossey-Bass, 1982.

Auletta, Gale S. and Terry Jones. "Reconstituting the Inner Circle." *American Behavioral Scientist* 34 (1990): 137-152.

Baker, Betsy and Mary Ellen Litzinger, eds. *The Evolving Educational Mission of the Library*. Chicago: Association of College and Research Libraries, 1992.

Bensimon, Estela M. and William G. Tierney. "Shaping the Multicultural Campus; Strategies for Administrators." *College Board Review* 166 (1992/93): 4-7, 30.

Bents, Mary and Catherine Haugen. "An Enrollment Management Model for Increasing Diversity." *College and University* 67 (1992): 195-201.

Boissé, Joseph A. and Connie V. Dowell. "Increasing Minority Librarians in Academic Research Libraries." *Library Journal* 112 (1987): 52-54.

Boyer, Ernest L. *College: The Undergraduate Experience in America*. New York: Harper and Row, 1987.

_____. *Tribal Colleges; Shaping the Future of Native America.*
Lawrenceville, NJ: Carnegie Foundation for the Advancement of
Teaching, 1989.

Brown, Lorene. "Student Admission and Multicultural Recruitment."
Journal of Library Administration 16 (1992): 109-122.

Buttlar, Lois and William Caynon. "Recruitment of Librarians into the
Profession: The Minority Perspective." *Library and Information
Science Research* 14 (1992): 259-280.

Cage, Mary Crystal. "Fewer Students Get Bachelor's Degrees in 4
Years, Study Finds." *Chronicle of Higher Education* (15 July
1992), A29-A32.

California. Legislature. Joint Committee for Review of the Master Plan
for Higher Education. *California Faces...California's Future;
Education for Citizenship in a Multicultural Democracy.* Sacramento: Joint Legislative Publications Office, 1989.

Carnegie Foundation for the Advancement of Teaching. "Native
Americans and Higher Education: New Mood of Optimism."
Change 22 (1990): 27-30.

Center for Policy Development. *Adrift in a Sea of Change; California's
Public Libraries Struggle to Meet the Information Needs of
Multicultural Communities.* Sacramento: California State Library,
1990.

Chadley, Otis A. "Addressing Cultural Diversity in Academic and
Research Libraries." *College and Research Libraries* 53 (1992):
206-214.

Cheng, Li-Rong Lilly. "Recognizing Diversity; A Need for a Paradigm
Shift." *American Behavioral Scientist* 34 (1990): 263-278.

Chronicle of Higher Education. *The Almanac of Higher Education.*
Chicago: University of Chicago Press, 1992.

Cleveland, Harlan. *The Knowledge Executive*. New York:E.P. Dutton, 1985.

Cope, Johnnye and Evelyn Black. "New Library Orientation for International Students." *College Teaching* 33 (1985): 159-162.

Davis, Hiram L. *MSU Idea: Library Planning Program Report*. East Lansing, MI: Michigan State University Libraries, 1990.

De los Santos, Alfredo and Richard C. Richardson. "Ten Principles for Good Institution Practice in Removing Race/Ethnicity as a Factor in College Completion." *Educational Record* 69 (1988): 43-46.

Dunn, Rita. "Learning Styles of the Multiculturally Diverse." *Emergency Librarian* 20 (1993): 24-32.

Dyson, Allan J. "Reaching Out for Outreach; A University Library Develops a New Position to Serve the School's Multicultural Students." *American Libraries* 20 (1989): 952-954.

Edwards, Ronald G. "Multiculturalism and Its Link to Quality Education and Democracy." *MultiCultural Review* 2 (1993): 12-14.

Evangelauf, Jean. "Number of Minority Students in College Rose 9% from 1990 to 1991, U. S. Reports." *Chronicle of Higher Education* (20 January 1993), A30.

Fink, Deborah. "Diverse Thinking: Pushing the Boundaries of Bibliographic Instruction" (paper presented at the Association of College and Research Libraries' preconference, *Cultural Diversity and Higher Education*, Atlanta, GA, 28 June 1991).

Fleming, Jacqueline. *Blacks in College*. San Francisco: Jossey-Bass, 1985.

Frederickson, H. George. "Public Administration and Social Equity." *Public Administration Review* 50 (1990): 228-237.

Freiband, Susan J. "Multicultural Issues and Concerns in Library Education." *Journal of Library and Information Science* 33 (1992): 287-294.

Fullilove, Robert E. and Philip Uri Treisman. "Mathematics Achievement Among African American Undergraduates at the University of California, Berkeley: An Evaluation of the Mathematics Workshop Program." *Journal of Negro Education* 59 (1990): 463-478.

Gaff, Jerry G. "Beyond Politics; the Educational Issues Inherent in Multicultural Education." *Change* 24 (1992): 31-35.

Gamson, Zelda, Marvin Peterson, and Robert Blackburn. "Stages in the Response of White Colleges and Universities to Black Students." *Journal of Higher Education* 51 (1980): 255-267.

Gerhard, Kristin H. and Jeanne M.K. Boydston. "A Library Committee on Diversity and Its Role in a Library Diversity Program." *College and Research Libraries* 54 (1993): 335-343.

Glaviano, Cliff and R. Errol Lam. "Academic Libraries and Affirmative Action: Approaching Cultural Diversity in the 1990s." *College and Research Libraries* 51 (1990): 513-523.

Gollop, Claudia J. "Selection and Acquisition of Multicultural Materials at the Libraries of the City University of New York." *Urban Academic Librarian* 8 (1991/1992): 20-29.

Green, James. *Cultural Awareness in the Human Services*. Englewood Cliffs, NJ: Prentice-Hall, 1982.

Greenfield, Louise, Susan Johnston, and Karen Williams. "Educating the World: Training Library Staff to Communicate Effectively with International Students." *Journal of Academic Librarianship* 12 (1986): 227-231.

Greenland, Annette E. "Responsiveness to Adult Undergraduates in a Traditional Land-Grant University; An Institution-Wide Assessment." *Equity and Excellence* 24 (1989): 13-19.

Hall, Patrick A. "Peanuts: A Note on Intercultural Communication." *Journal of Academic Librarianship* 18 (1992): 211-213.

_____. "The Role of Affectivity in Instructing People of Color: Some Implications for Bibliographic Instruction." *Library Trends* 39 (1991): 316-326.

Hefner, James A. and Lelia G. Rhodes. "Excellence in Education: Libraries Facilitating Learning for Minority Students." In *Libraries and the Search for Academic Excellence*, ed. Patricia Senn Breivik and Robert Wedgeworth, 57-74. Metuchen NJ: Scarecrow Press, 1988.

Hoffman, Irene and Oprista Popa. "Library Orientation and Instruction for International Students: The University of California-Davis Experience." *RQ* 25 (1986): 356-360.

Hsia, Jayjia. *Asian Americans in Higher Education and at Work.* Hillsdale, NJ: Lawrence Erlbaum Associates, 1988.

Hsia, Jayjia and Marsha Hirano-Nakanishi. "The Demographics of Diversity: Asian Americans and Higher Education." *Change* 21 (1989): 20-27.

Huston, Mary M. "Building New Relationships and Valuing Diversity Through the Information Seeking Process: From Picture Books to Hyper Space." *MultiCultural Review* 1 (1992): 8-19.

_____. "May I Introduce You: Teaching Culturally Diverse End-Users Through Everyday Information Seeking Experiences." *Reference Services Review* 17 (1989): 7-11.

Jackson, Kenneth W. and L. Alex Swan. "Institutional and Individual Factors Affecting Black Undergraduate Student Performance." In *College in Black and White*, ed. Walter R. Allen, Edgar G. Epps, and Nesha Z. Haniff, 127-141. Albany: State University of New York Press, 1991.

Jacobson, Frances F. "Bibliographic Instruction and International Students." *Illinois Libraries* 70 (1988): 628-633.

Janes, Phoebe and Ellen Meltzer. "Origins and Attitudes: Training Reference Librarians for a Pluralistic World." *Reference Librarian* no. 30 (1990): 145-155.

Johnston, William B. *Workforce 2000; Work and Workers for the 21st Century*. Indianapolis, IN: Hudson Institute, 1987.

Jones, Kay F. "Multicultural Diversity and the Academic Library." *Urban Academic Librarian* 8 (1990/1991): 14-22.

Josey, E.J. "Education for Library Services to Cultural Minorities." *Journal of Multicultural Librarianship* 5 (1991): 104-111.

Keller, Gary D., James R. Deneen, and Raphael J. Magallan, eds. *Assessment and Access; Hispanics in Higher Education*. Albany: State University of New York Press, 1991.

Kflu, Tesfai and Mary A. Loomba. "Academic Libraries and the Culturally Diverse Student Population." *College and Research Libraries News* 51 (1990): 524-527.

Kline, Laura S. and Catherine M. Rod. "Library Orientation Programs for Foreign Students: A Survey." *RQ* 24 (1984): 210-216.

Kravitz, Rhonda Rios, Adelia Lines, and Vivian Sykes. "Serving the Emerging Majority: Documenting Their Voices." *Library Administration and Management* 5 (1991): 184-188.

Lam, R. Errol. "The Reference Interview: Some Intercultural Considerations." *RQ* 27 (1988): 390-395.

Lang, Marvel. "Barriers to Blacks' Educational Achievement in Higher Education." *Journal of Black Studies* 22 (1992): 510-522.

Levine, Arthur. "The Meaning of Diversity." *Change* 23 (1991): 4-5.

_____. "A Time to Act." *Change* 24 (1992): 4-5.

_____, ed. *Shaping Higher Education's Future; Demographic Realities and Opportunities, 1990-2000*. San Francisco: Jossey-Bass, 1989.

Levine, Arthur and Jeanette Cureton. "The Quiet Revolution; Eleven Facts About Multiculturalism and the Curriculum." *Change* 24 (1992): 25-29.

Liestman, Daniel. "The Disadvantaged Minority Student and the Academic Library." *Urban Academic Librarian* 8 (1991/1992): 13-19.

Liu, Ziming. "Difficulties and Characteristics of Students from Developing Countries in Using American Libraries." *College and Research Libraries* 54 (1993): 25-31.

Llabre, Maria Magdalena. "Time as a Factor in the Cognitive Test Performance of Latino College Students." In *Assessment and Access; Hispanics in Higher Education*, ed. Gary D. Keller, James R. Deneen, and Raphael J. Magallan, 95-104. Albany: State University of New York Press, 1991.

Loo, Chalsa and Garry Rolison. "Alienation of Ethnic Minority Students at a Predominantly White University." *Journal of Higher Education* 57 (1986): 58-77.

MacAdam, Barbara and Darlene P. Nichols. "Peer Information Counseling: An Academic Library Program for Minority Students." *Journal of Academic Librarianship* 15 (1989): 204-209.

Mallinckrodt, Brent and William F. Sedlacek. "Student Retention and the Use of Campus Facilities by Race." *NASPA Journal* 24 (1987): 28-32.

McKenna, Teresa and Flora Ida Ortiz, eds. *The Broken Web: The Educational Experience of Hispanic American Women*. Berkeley, CA: The Tomas Rivera Center and Floricanto Press, 1988.

McPherson, Michael S. "Value Conflicts in American Higher Education." *Journal of Higher Education* 54 (1983): 243-278.

Mensching, Teresa B. *Reaching and Teaching Diverse Library User Groups*. Ann Arbor, MI: Pierian Press, 1989.

Miller, Carol A. "Minority Student Achievement: A Comprehensive Perspective." *Journal of Developmental Education* 13 (1990): 6-11.

Mitchell-Powell, Brenda. "Color Me Multicultural." *MultiCultural Review* 1 (1992): 15-17.

Mood, Terry Ann. "Foreign Students and the Academic Library." *RQ* 22 (1982): 176-180.

Moorhead, Wendy. "Ignorance Was Our Excuse." *College and Research Libraries News* 47 (1986): 585-587.

Nettles, Michael T. "Racial Similarities and Differences in the Predictors of College Student Attainment." In *College in Black and White*, ed. Walter R. Allen, Edgar G. Epps, and Nesha Z. Haniff, 75-91. Albany: State University of New York Press, 1991.

_____, ed. *Toward Black Undergraduate Student Equality in American Higher Education*. Westport, CT: Greenwood Press, 1988.

Odell, Morgan and Jere J. Mock, eds. *A Crucial Agenda: Making Colleges and Universities Work Better for Minority Students*. Boulder, CO: Western Interstate Commission for Higher Education, 1989.

Olivas, Michael A., ed. *Latino College Students*. New York: Teachers College Press, 1986.

Oppelt, Norman T. "Cultural Values and Behaviors Common Among Tribal American Indians: A Resource for Student Service Administrators." *NASPA Journal* 26 (1989): 167-179.

_____. *The Tribally Controlled Indian College; The Beginnings of Self Determination in American Indian Education*. Tsaile, AZ: Navajo Community College Press, 1990.

Padilla, Raymond V. "Assessing Heuristic Knowledge to Enhance College Students' Success." In *Assessment and Access; Hispanics in Higher Education*, ed. Gary D. Keller, James R. Deneen, and Raphael J. Magallan, 81-92. Albany: State University of New York Press, 1991.

Pastine, Maureen and Linda Wilson. "Curriculum Reform: The Role of Academic Libraries." In *The Evolving Educational Mission of the Library*, ed. Betsy Baker and Mary Ellen Litzinger, 90-108. Chicago: Association of College and Research Libraries, 1992.

Payne, Judith. *Public Libraries Face California's Ethnic and Racial Diversity*. Santa Monica, CA: RAND Corporation, 1988.

Piele, Linda J. and Brian Yamel. "Reference Assistance Project at the University of Wisconsin-Parkside." *College and Research Libraries News* 43 (1982): 83-84.

Porter, Oscar F. *Undergraduate Completion and Persistence at Four-Year Colleges and Universities*. Washington, DC: National Institute of Independent Colleges and Universities, 1990.

Quezada, Shelley. "Mainstreaming Library Services to Multicultural Populations: The Evolving Tapestry." *Wilson Library Bulletin* 66 (1992): 28-29, 120.

Rader, Hannelore and William Coons. "Information Literacy: One Response to the New Decade." In *The Evolving Educational Mission of the Library*, ed. Betsy Baker and Mary Ellen Litzinger, 109-127. Chicago: Association of College and Research Libraries, 1992.

Resta, Paul. "Organizing Education for Minorities: Enhancing Minority Access and Use of the New Information Technologies in Higher Education." *Education and Computing* 8 (1992): 119-127.

Richardson, Richard C. and Elizabeth Fisk Skinner. *Achieving Quality and Diversity; Universities in a Multicultural Society.* New York: Macmillan, 1991.

Richardson, Richard C. and Louis W. Bender. *Fostering Minority Access and Achievement in Higher Education.* San Francisco: Jossey-Bass, 1987.

Robbins, Steven B. and Laura C. Smith. "Enhancement Programs for Entering University Majority and Minority Freshmen." *Journal of Counseling and Development* 71 (1993): 510-514.

Saltzstein, Grace Hall. "Conceptualizing Bureaucratic Responsiveness." *Administration and Society* 17 (1985): 283-306.

Scarborough, Katharine T. A. "Collections for the Emerging Majority." *Library Journal* 116 (1991): 44-47.

_____, ed. *Developing Library Collections for California's Emerging Majority.* Berkeley, CA: Bay Area Library and Information System and the School of Library and Information Studies, University of California, Berkeley, 1990.

Schmidt, Ronald J. "Cultural Pluralism and Public Administration: The Role of Community-Based Organizations." *American Review of Public Administration* 18 (1988): 189-202.

Sharp, Elaine B. *Citizen Demand-Making in the Urban Context.* [Tuscaloosa:] University of Alabama Press, 1986.

_____. "Responsiveness in Urban Service Delivery." *Administration and Society* 13 (1981): 33-50.

Singh, B.R. "Cognitive Styles, Cultural Pluralism and Effective Teaching and Learning." *International Review of Education* 34 (1988): 355-370.

Smith, Daryl G. *The Challenge of Diversity: Involvement or Alienation in the Academy?* Report No. 5. Washington, DC: School of Education and Human Development, George Washington University, 1989.

_____. "Embracing Diversity as a Central Campus Goal." *Academe* 76 (1990): 29-33.

State Higher Education Executive Officers. *A Difference of Degrees: State Initiatives to Improve Minority Student Achievement*. Denver: State Higher Education Executive Officers, 1987.

Stoecker, Judith, Ernest T. Pascarella, and Lee M. Wolfe. "Persistence in Higher Education: A 9-Year Test of a Theoretical Model." *Journal of College Student Development* 29 (1988): 196-209.

Stoffle, Carla. "A New Library for the New Undergraduate." *Library Journal* 115 (1990): 47-51.

Sue, Derald Wing, Patricia Arrendondo, and Roderick J. McDavis. "Multicultural Counseling Competencies and Standards." *Journal of Multicultural Counseling and Development* 20 (1992): 64-88.

Suzuki, Bob H. "Asian Americans as the 'Model Minority.'" *Change* 21 (1989): 13-19.

Sykes, Vivian. "Reference Service to the Multicultural Library User." *CARL Newsletter* 12 (1988): 2-3.

Tarin, Patricia. "RAND Misses the Point: A Minority Report." *Library Journal* 113 (1988): 31-34.

Terrell, Melvin C., ed. *Diversity, Disunity, and Campus Community*. [Washington, DC:] National Association of Student Personnel Administrators, 1992.

Thoeny, A. Robert. "Strategies for Action." In *Toward Black Undergraduate Student Equality in American Higher Education*, ed. Michael T. Nettles, 197-201. Westport, CT: Greenwood Press, 1988.

Tinto, Vincent. *Leaving College; Rethinking the Causes and Cures of Student Attrition*. Chicago, IL: University of Chicago Press, 1987.

Trujillo, Roberto G. and David C. Weber. "Academic Library Responses to Cultural Diversity: A Position Paper for the 1990s." *Journal of Academic Librarianship* 17 (1991): 157-161.

U.S. Department of Education. "Bachelors Degrees Conferred by Racial and Ethnic Group, 1990-91." *Chronicle of Higher Education* (2 June 1993), A25.

University of Michigan Library. *Point of Intersection: The University Library and the Pluralistic Campus Community*. Ann Arbor, MI: The University of Michigan Library, 1988.

_____. *Point of Intersection II: The University Library Moves Toward Diversity*. Ann Arbor, MI: The University of Michigan Library, 1990.

Welch, Janet E. and R. Errol Lam. "The Library and the Pluralistic Campus in the Year 2000: Implications for Administrators." *Library Administration and Management* 5 (1991): 212-216.

Wertheimer, M. Leonard, ed. "Library Services to Ethnocultural Minorities." *Library Trends* 29 (1980): 175-273.

Western Interstate Commission for Higher Education and The College Board. *The Road to College; Educational Progress by Race and Ethnicity*. Boulder, CO: Western Interstate Commission for Higher Education, 1991.

Wilkerson, Margaret B. "Beyond the Graveyard; Engaging Faculty Involvement." *Change* 24 (1992): 59-63.

Wilson, Lizabeth A. "Changing Users: Bibliographic Instruction for Whom?" In *The Evolving Educational Mission of the Library*, ed. Betsy Baker and Mary Ellen Litzinger, 20-53. Chicago: Association of College and Research Libraries, 1992.

Woolbright, Cynthia, ed. *Valuing Diversity on Campus: A Multicultural Approach*. Bloomington, IN: Association of College Unions-International, 1989.

Wright, Joyce C. "Recruitment and Retention of Minorities in Academic Libraries: A Plan for Action for the 1990s." *Illinois Libraries* 72 (1990): 621-625.

Yin, Robert K. *Case Study Research; Design and Methods*. Newbury Park, CA: Sage Publications, 1989.

Zoglin, Mary Lou. "Community College Responsiveness: Myth or Reality?" *Journal of Higher Education* 52 (1981): 415-426.

INDEX

255

ABOUT THE AUTHOR

REBECCA R. MARTIN (B.A., University of California, Santa Cruz; M.A., San Jose State University; D.P.A., University of Southern California) is the Director of Libraries and Media Services and Library Professor at the University of Vermont. After holding administrative positions in hospital libraries, Dr. Martin became Head of the Biology Library at the University of California, Berkeley, and then Associate Director for User Services and Collection Development at San Jose State University. Active in national and regional library associations, she has served on the Board of Directors of the Library Administration and Management Association and as President of the California Academic and Research Librarians. Previous publications in professional journals have covered topics of concern to all librarians, including public service, library instruction, and library automation. At UVM, Dr. Martin has been active in the development of university-wide efforts to create a multicultural campus. Recently, she also received an additional appointment to teach in the Public Administration Department.